ON WRITING WELL

ON WRITING WELL

AN INFORMAL GUIDE TO WRITING NONFICTION

WILLIAM ZINSSER

SECOND EDITION

Harper & Row, Publishers

New York

Cambridge
Hagerstown
Philadelphia
San Francisco

1817

London
Mexico City
São Paulo
Sydney

ON WRITING WELL: *An Informal Guide to Writing Nonfiction* (Second Edition). Copyright © 1980 by William K. Zinsser. All rights reserved. Printed in the United States of America. No part of this book may be used or reproduced in any manner whatsoever without written permission except in the case of brief quotations embodied in critical articles and reviews. For information address Harper & Row, Publishers, Inc., 10 East 53rd Street, New York, N.Y. 10022. Published simultaneously in Canada by Fitzhenry & Whiteside Limited, Toronto.

Designed by Sidney Feinberg

Library of Congress Cataloging in Publication Data

Zinsser, William Knowlton.
  On writing well.
  Bibliography: p.
  Includes index.
    1. English language—Rhetoric. 2. Exposition
(Rhetoric) 3. Prose literature—Technique.
  I. Title.
PE1429.Z5   808'.042   79-2641
ISBN 0-06-014804-7 (Trade ed.) 80 81 82 83 10 9 8 7 6 5 4 3 2 1
ISBN 0-06-47396-7 (College ed.) 80 81 82 83 10 9 8 7 6 5 4 3 2 1

    81 82 83 10 9 8 7 6 5 4 3

Contents

Preface to the Second Edition

This book grew out of a course that I originated and taught at Yale in writing nonfiction, which in turn grew out of a long career of practicing the craft in a multitude of forms for one newspaper—the *New York Herald Tribune*—and a variety of magazines. Since it was first published in 1976 I have heard from hundreds of readers and talked to many groups of writers, editors, teachers, educators, businessmen and other people who have found the book helpful. They raised questions about writing, or about teaching writing, that I had not encountered before or that I just didn't think of including.

In this Second Edition I have tried to answer the questions that were asked most often and to incorporate many points that have since occurred to me. Quite a few of my additions have been woven into the text where they seemed to fit most naturally. Often they are just a few sentences to amplify an earlier point. But many longer stretches of writing are entirely new. I have added to the chapter on "Usage" a section on jargon, one of the most troublesome areas (I gather) for writers and teachers who know that jargon is swamping the language but don't know if any of it is acceptable. I have added new entries to the chapter on "Bits & Pieces." The chapter on "Sports" has been expanded to note the many new factors that have changed this major area of American life. A once-innocent world has suddenly become far more complex for the nonfiction writer.

I have written a new chapter (Chapter 15) for all the people who have to do a certain amount of writing in their job —men and women who work for businesses, school systems, law firms, government agencies and other institutions. Much of what is written in everyday American life is cold, pompous and impenetrable. I have tried to demystify the process and to show that institutions can be made human. I have also greatly expanded the chapter on "Humor." In the First Edition this chapter was devoted largely to demonstrating that humor is a valuable tool for making a serious point about current issues. Since then I have twice taught a course at Yale in humor writing and have learned far more about its methods.

On Writing Well is a highly personal book—one man's opinions and prejudices. But I have included excerpts from the work of many other writers to show how they solved a particular problem. I also wanted to indicate the wide range of possibilities that are open to anyone trying to write nonfiction, both in subject and in tone of voice. Some outdated excerpts, references and usages that were in the First Edition have been dropped or replaced with fresher examples. I have also added a dozen writers who were not along on the previous ride.

My purpose is not to teach good nonfiction, or good journalism, but to teach good English that can be put to those uses. Don't assume that bad English can still be good journalism. It can't. All the writers quoted in this book were chosen because they write good English, no matter how "popular" the journal that they originally wrote for. They never talk down to the reader. They are true to themselves and to what they want to say and to how they want to say it. They are vastly dissimilar in style and in personality, but they have all learned the one lesson that must be learned: how to control their material. You can, too.

W.Z.

New York
October 1979

ON WRITING WELL

PART I

1. The Transaction

Five or six years ago a school in Connecticut held "a day devoted to the arts," and I was asked if I would come and talk about writing as a vocation. When I arrived I found that a second speaker had been invited—Dr. Brock (as I'll call him), a surgeon who had recently begun to write and had sold some stories to national magazines. He was going to talk about writing as an avocation. That made us a panel, and we sat down to face a crowd of student newspaper editors and reporters, English teachers and parents, all eager to learn the secrets of our glamorous work.

Dr. Brock was dressed in a bright red jacket, looking vaguely Bohemian, as authors are supposed to look, and the first question went to him. What was it like to be a writer?

He said it was tremendous fun. Coming home from an arduous day at the hospital, he would go straight to his yellow pad and write his tensions away. The words just flowed. It was easy.

I then said that writing wasn't easy and it wasn't fun. It was hard and lonely, and the words seldom just flowed.

Next Dr. Brock was asked if it was important to rewrite. Absolutely not, he said. "Let it all hang out," and whatever form the sentences take will reflect the writer at his most natural.

I then said that rewriting is the essence of writing. I pointed out that professional writers rewrite their sentences repeatedly and then rewrite what they have rewritten. I mentioned that E. B. White and James Thurber were known to rewrite their pieces eight or nine times.

"What do you do on days when it isn't going well?" Dr. Brock was asked. He said he just stopped writing and put the work aside for a day when it would go better.

I then said that the professional writer must establish a daily schedule and stick to it. I said that writing is a craft, not an art, and that the man who runs away from his craft because he lacks inspiration is fooling himself. He is also going broke.

"What if you're feeling depressed or unhappy?" a student asked. "Won't that affect your writing?"

Probably it will, Dr. Brock replied. Go fishing. Take a walk.

Probably it won't, I said. If your job is to write every day, you learn to do it like any other job.

A student asked if we found it useful to circulate in the literary world. Dr. Brock said that he was greatly enjoying his new life as a man of letters, and he told several lavish stories of being taken to lunch by his publisher and his agent at Manhattan restaurants where writers and editors gather. I said that professional writers are solitary drudges who seldom see other writers.

"Do you put symbolism in your writing?" a student asked me.

"Not if I can help it," I replied. I have an unbroken record of missing the deeper meaning in any story, play or movie, and as for dance and mime, I have never had even a remote notion of what is being conveyed.

"I *love* symbols!" Dr. Brock exclaimed, and he described with gusto the joys of weaving them through his work.

So the morning went, and it was a revelation to all of us. At the end Dr. Brock told me he was enormously interested in my answers—it had never occurred to him that writing could be hard. I told him I was just as interested in *his* answers—it had never occurred to me that writing could be easy. (Maybe I should take up surgery on the side.)

As for the students, anyone might think that we left them bewildered. But in fact we probably gave them a broader glimpse of the writing process than if only one of us had talked. For of course there isn't any "right" way to do such intensely personal work. There are all kinds of writers and all kinds of methods, and any method that helps somebody to say what he wants to say is the right method for him.

Some people write by day, others by night. Some people need silence, others turn on the radio. Some write by hand, some by typewriter, some by talking into a tape recorder. Some people write their first draft in one long burst and then revise; others can't write the second paragraph until they have fiddled endlessly with the first.

But all of them are vulnerable and all of them are tense. They are driven by a compulsion to put some part of themselves on paper, and yet they don't just write what comes naturally. They sit down to commit an act of literature, and the self who emerges on paper is a far stiffer person than the one who sat down. The problem is to find the real man or woman behind all the tension.

For ultimately the product that any writer has to sell is not his subject, but who he is. I often find myself reading with interest about a topic that I never thought would interest me —some unusual scientific quest, for instance. What holds me is the enthusiasm of the writer for his field. How was he drawn into it? What emotional baggage did he bring along? How did it change his life? It is not necessary to want to spend a year alone at Walden Pond to become deeply involved with a man who did.

This is the personal transaction that is at the heart of good nonfiction writing. Out of it come two of the most important qualities that this book will go in search of: humanity and warmth. Good writing has an aliveness that keeps the reader reading from one paragraph to the next, and it's not a question of gimmicks to "personalize" the author. It's a question of using the English language in a way that will achieve the greatest strength and the least clutter.

Can such principles be taught? Maybe not. But most of them can be learned.

2. Simplicity

Clutter is the disease of American writing. We are a society strangling in unnecessary words, circular constructions, pompous frills and meaningless jargon.

Who can understand the viscous language of everyday American commerce and enterprise: the business letter, the interoffice memo, the corporation report, the notice from the bank explaining its latest "simplified" statement? What member of an insurance or medical plan can decipher the brochure that tells him what his costs and benefits are? What father or mother can put together a child's toy—on Christmas Eve or any other eve—from the instructions on the box? Our national tendency is to inflate and thereby sound important. The airline pilot who wakes us to announce that he is presently anticipating experiencing considerable weather wouldn't dream of saying that there's a storm ahead and it may get bumpy. The sentence is too simple—there must be something wrong with it.

But the secret of good writing is to strip every sentence to its cleanest components. Every word that serves no function, every long word that could be a short word, every adverb which carries the same meaning that is already in the verb, every passive construction that leaves the reader unsure of who is doing what—these are the thousand and one adulterants that weaken the strength of a sentence. And they usually occur, ironically, in proportion to education and rank.

During the late 1960s the president of a major university wrote a letter to mollify the alumni after a spell of campus unrest. "You are probably aware," he began, "that we have been experiencing very considerable potentially explosive expressions of dissatisfaction on issues only partially related." He meant that the students had been hassling them about different things. I was far more upset by the president's English than by the students' potentially explosive expressions of dissatisfaction. I would have preferred the presidential approach taken by Franklin D. Roosevelt when he tried to convert into English his own government's memos, such as this blackout order of 1942:

> Such preparations shall be made as will completely obscure all Federal buildings and non-Federal buildings occupied by the Federal government during an air raid for any period of time from visibility by reason of internal or external illumination.

"Tell them," Roosevelt said, "that in buildings where they have to keep the work going to put something across the windows."

Simplify, simplify. Thoreau said it, as we are so often reminded, and no American writer more consistently practiced what he preached. Open *Walden* to any page and you will find a man saying in a plain and orderly way what is on his mind:

> I love to be alone. I never found the companion that was so companionable as solitude. We are for the most part more lonely when we go abroad among men than when we stay in our chambers. A man thinking or working is always alone, let him be where he will. Solitude is not measured by the miles of space that intervene between a man and his fellows. The really diligent student in one of the crowded

hives of Cambridge College is as solitary as a dervish in the desert.

How can the rest of us achieve such enviable freedom from clutter? The answer is to clear our heads of clutter. Clear thinking becomes clear writing: one can't exist without the other. It is impossible for a muddy thinker to write good English. He may get away with it for a paragraph or two, but soon the reader will be lost, and there is no sin so grave, for he will not easily be lured back.

Who is this elusive creature the reader? He is a person with an attention span of about twenty seconds. He is assailed on every side by forces competing for his time: by newspapers and magazines, by television and radio and stereo, by his wife and children and pets, by his house and his yard and all the gadgets that he has bought to keep them spruce, and by that most potent of competitors, sleep. The man snoozing in his chair with an unfinished magazine open on his lap is a man who was being given too much unnecessary trouble by the writer.

It won't do to say that the snoozing reader is too dumb or too lazy to keep pace with the train of thought. My sympathies are with him. If the reader is lost, it is generally because the writer has not been careful enough to keep him on the path.

This carelessness can take any number of forms. Perhaps a sentence is so excessively cluttered that the reader, hacking his way through the verbiage, simply doesn't know what it means. Perhaps a sentence has been so shoddily constructed that the reader could read it in any of several ways. Perhaps the writer has switched pronouns in mid-sentence, or has switched tenses, so the reader loses track of who is talking or when the action took place. Perhaps Sentence B is not a logical sequel to Sentence A—the writer, in whose head the connection is clear, has not bothered to provide the missing link. Perhaps the writer has used an important word incorrectly by not taking the trouble to look it up. He may think that "sanguine" and "sanguinary"

5 --

is too dumb or too lazy to keep pace with the ~~writer's~~ train
of thought. My sympathies are ~~entirely~~ with him. ~~He's not~~
~~so dumb.~~ If the reader is lost, it is generally because the
writer ~~of the article~~ has not been careful enough to keep
him on the ~~proper~~ path.

This carelessness can take any number of ~~different~~ forms.
Perhaps a sentence is so excessively ~~long and~~ cluttered that
the reader, hacking his way through ~~all~~ the verbiage, simply
doesn't know what *it* ~~the writer~~ means. Perhaps a sentence has
been so shoddily constructed that the reader could read it in
any of *several* ~~two or three different~~ ways. ~~He thinks he knows what~~
~~the writer is trying to say, but he's not sure.~~ Perhaps the
writer has switched pronouns in mid-sentence, or ~~perhaps he~~
has switched tenses, so the reader loses track of who is
talking ~~to whom~~ or ~~exactly~~ when the action took place. Perhaps Sentence B is not a logical sequel to Sentence A -- the
writer, in whose head the connection is ~~perfectly~~ clear, has
not *bothered to provide* ~~given enough thought to providing~~ the missing link. Perhaps the writer has used an important word incorrectly by not
taking the trouble to look it up ~~and make sure.~~ He may think
that "sanguine" and "sanguinary" mean the same thing, but
~~I can assure you that~~ the difference is a bloody big one ~~to the~~
~~reader.~~ *The reader* ~~He~~ can only ~~try to~~ infer ~~what~~ (speaking of big differences) what the writer is trying to imply.

Faced with *these* ~~such a variety of~~ obstacles, the reader
is at first a remarkably tenacious bird. He ~~tends to~~ blame*s*
himself. ~~He~~ obviously missed something, ~~he thinks,~~ and he goes
back over the mystifying sentence, or over the whole paragraph,

6 --

piecing it out like an ancient rune, making guesses and moving

on. But he won't do this for long. ~~He will soon run out of~~

~~patience.~~ (The writer is making him work too hard ~~--harder~~

~~than he should have to work --~~ (and the reader will look for

~~a writer,~~ **one** who is better at his craft.

The writer must therefore constantly ask himself: What am

I trying to say ~~in this sentence?~~ (Surprisingly often, he

doesn't know.) ~~And~~ Then he must look at what he has ~~just~~

written and ask: Have I said it? Is it clear to someone

encountering ~~who is coming upon~~ the subject for the first time? If it's

not ~~clear,~~ it is because some fuzz has worked its way into the

machinery. The clear writer is a person ~~who is~~ clear-headed

enough to see this stuff for what it is: fuzz.

I don't mean ~~to suggest~~ that some people are born

clear-headed and are therefore natural writers, whereas

others ~~other people~~ are naturally fuzzy and will ~~therefore~~ never write

well. Thinking clearly is **a** ~~an entirely~~ conscious act that the

writer must **force** ~~keep forcing~~ upon himself, just as if he were

embarking ~~starting out~~ on any other ~~kind of~~ project that **requires** ~~calls for~~ logic:

adding up a laundry list or doing an algebra problem ~~or playing~~

~~chess.~~ Good writing doesn't ~~just~~ come naturally, though most

people obviously think **it does.** ~~it's as easy as walking.~~ The professional

Two pages of the final manuscript of this chapter. Although they look like a first draft, they have already been rewritten and retyped—like almost every other page—four or five times. With each rewrite I try to make what I have written tighter, stronger and more precise, eliminating every element that is not doing useful work, until at last I have a clean copy for the printer. Then I go over it once more, reading it aloud, and am always amazed at how much clutter can still be profitably cut.

mean the same thing, but the difference is a bloody big one. The reader can only infer (speaking of big differences) what the writer is trying to imply.

Faced with these obstacles, the reader is at first a remarkably tenacious bird. He blames himself—he obviously missed something, and he goes back over the mystifying sentence, or over the whole paragraph, piecing it out like an ancient rune, making guesses and moving on. But he won't do this for long. The writer is making him work too hard, and the reader will look for one who is better at his craft.

The writer must therefore constantly ask himself: What am I trying to say? Surprisingly often, he doesn't know. Then he must look at what he has written and ask: Have I said it? Is it clear to someone encountering the subject for the first time? If it's not, it is because some fuzz has worked its way into the machinery. The clear writer is a person clear-headed enough to see this stuff for what it is: fuzz.

I don't mean that some people are born clear-headed and are therefore natural writers, whereas others are naturally fuzzy and will never write well. Thinking clearly is a conscious act that the writer must force upon himself, just as if he were embarking on any other project that requires logic: adding up a laundry list or doing an algebra problem. Good writing doesn't come naturally, though most people obviously think it does. The professional writer is forever being bearded by strangers who say that they'd like to "try a little writing sometime" when they retire from their real profession. Good writing takes self-discipline and, very often, self-knowledge.

Many writers, for instance, can't stand to throw anything away. Their sentences are littered with words that mean essentially the same thing and with phrases which make a point that is implicit in what they have already said. When students give me these littered sentences I beg them to select from the surfeit of words the few that most precisely fit what they want to say. Choose one, I plead, from among the three almost identical adjectives. Get rid of the unnecessary adverbs. Eliminate "in a funny sort of way" and other such qualifiers—they do no useful work.

The students look stricken—I am taking all their wonderful words away. I am only taking their superfluous words away, leaving what is organic and strong.

"But," one of my worst offenders confessed, "I never can get rid of anything—you should see my room." (I didn't take him up on the offer.) "I have two lamps where I only need one, but I can't decide which one I like better, so I keep them both." He went on to enumerate his duplicated or unnecessary objects, and over the weeks ahead I went on throwing away his duplicated and unnecessary words. By the end of the term—a term that he found acutely painful—his sentences were clean.

"I've had to change my whole approach to writing," he told me. "Now I have to *think* before I start every sentence and I have to *think* about every word." The very idea amazed him. Whether his room also looked better I never found out.

Writing is hard work. A clear sentence is no accident. Very few sentences come out right the first time, or the third. Keep thinking and rewriting until you say what you want to say.

3. Clutter

Fighting clutter is like fighting weeds—the writer is always slightly behind. New varieties sprout overnight, and by noon they are part of American speech. It only takes a John Dean testifying on TV to have everyone in the country saying "at this point in time" instead of "now."

Consider all the prepositions that are routinely draped onto verbs that don't need any help. Head up. Free up. Face up to. We no longer head committees. We head them up. We don't face problems anymore. We face up to them when we can free up a few minutes. A small detail, you may say—not worth bothering about. It *is* worth bothering about. The game is won or lost on hundreds of small details. Writing improves in direct ratio to the number of things we can keep out of it that shouldn't be there. "Up" in "free up" shouldn't be there. Can we picture anything being freed *up?* The writer of clean English must examine every word that he puts on paper. He will find a surprising number that don't serve any purpose.

Take the adjective "personal," as in "a personal friend of mine," "his personal feeling" or "her personal physician." It is typical of the words that can be eliminated nine times out of ten. The personal friend has come into the language to distinguish him from the business friend, thereby debasing not only language but friendship. Someone's feeling *is* his personal feeling—that's what "his" means. As for the personal physician, he is that man so often summoned to the dressing room of a stricken actress so that she won't have to be treated by the impersonal physician assigned to the theater. Someday I'd like to see him identified as "her doctor."

Or take those curious intervals of time like the short minute. "Twenty-two short minutes later she had won the final set." Minutes are minutes, physicians are physicians, friends are friends. The rest is clutter.

Clutter is the laborious phrase which has pushed out the short word that means the same thing. These locutions are a drag on energy and momentum. Even before John Dean gave us "at this point in time," people had stopped saying "now." They were saying "at the present time," or "currently," or "presently" (which means "soon"). Yet the idea can always be expressed by "now" to mean the immediate moment ("Now I can see him"), or by "today" to mean the historical present ("Today prices are high"), or simply by the verb "to be" ("It is raining"). There is no need to say, "At the present time we are experiencing precipitation."

Speaking of which, we are experiencing considerable difficulty getting *that* word out of the language now that it has lumbered in. Even your dentist will ask if you are experiencing any pain. If he were asking one of his own children he would say, "Does it hurt?" He would, in short, be himself. By using a more pompous phrase in his professional role he not only sounds more important; he blunts the painful edge of truth. It is the language of the airline stewardess demonstrating the oxygen mask that will drop down if the plane should somehow run out of air. "In the extremely unlikely possibility that the aircraft should experience such an eventuality," she begins—a phrase so oxygen-depriving in itself that we are prepared for any disaster, and even gasping death shall lose its sting. As for those "smoking materials" that she asks us to "kindly extinguish," I often wonder what materials are smoking. Maybe she thinks my coat and tie are on fire.

Clutter is the ponderous euphemism that turns a slum into a depressed socioeconomic area, a salesman into a marketing representative, a dumb kid into an underachiever and garbage collectors into waste disposal personnel. In New Canaan, Conn., the incinerator is now the "volume reduction plant." I hate to think what they call the town dump.

Clutter is the official language used by the American corporation—in the news release and the annual report—to hide its mistakes. When a big company recently announced that it was "decentralizing its organizational structure into major profit-centered businesses" and that "corporate staff services will be aligned under two senior vice-presidents" it meant that it had had a lousy year.

Clutter is the language of the interoffice memo ("The trend to mosaic communication is reducing the meaningfulness of concern about whether or not demographic segments differ in their tolerance of periodicity") and the language of computers ("We are offering functional digital programming options that have built-in parallel reciprocal capabilities with compatible third-generation contingencies and hardware").

Clutter is the language of the Pentagon throwing dust in the eyes of the populace by calling an invasion a "reinforced protective reaction strike" and by justifying its vast budgets on the need for "credible second-strike capability" and "counterforce deterrence." How can we grasp such vaporous double-talk? As George Orwell pointed out in "Politics and the English Language," an essay written in 1946 but cited frequently during the Vietnam years of Johnson and Nixon, "In our time, political speech and writing are largely the defense of the indefensible. . . . Thus political language has to consist largely of euphemism, question-begging and sheer cloudy vagueness." Orwell's warning that clutter is not just a nuisance but a deadly tool did not turn out to be inoperative. By the 1960s his words had come true in America.

I could go on quoting examples from various fields—every profession has its growing arsenal of jargon to fire at the layman and hurl him back from its walls. But the list would be depressing and the lesson tedious. The point of raising it now is to serve notice that clutter is the enemy, whatever form it takes. It slows the reader and robs the writer of his personality, making him seem pretentious.

Beware, then, of the long word that is no better than the short word: "numerous" (many), "facilitate" (ease), "individual" (man or woman), "remainder" (rest), "initial" (first), "implement" (do), "sufficient" (enough), "attempt" (try), "referred to as" (called), and hundreds more. Beware, too, of all the slippery new fad words for which the language already has equivalents: overview and quantify, paradigm and parameter, input and throughput, peer group and interface, private sector and public sector, optimize and maximize, prioritize and potentialize. They are all weeds that will smother what you write.

Nor are all the weeds so obvious. Just as insidious are the little growths of perfectly ordinary words with which we explain how we propose to go about our explaining, or which inflate a simple preposition or conjunction into a whole windy phrase.

"I might add," "It should be pointed out," "It is interesting to note that"—how many sentences begin with these dreary clauses announcing what the writer is going to do next? If you might add, add it. If it should be pointed out, point it out. If it is interesting to note, *make* it interesting. Being told that something is interesting is the surest way of tempting the reader to find it dull; are we not all stupefied by what follows when someone says, "This will interest you"? As for the inflated prepositions and conjunctions, they are the innumerable phrases like "with the possible exception of " (except), "for the reason that" (because), "he totally lacked the ability to" (he couldn't), "until such time as" (until), "for the purpose of " (for).

Clutter takes more forms than you can shake twenty sticks at. Prune it ruthlessly. Be grateful for everything that you can throw away. Re-examine each sentence that you put on paper. Is every word doing new and useful work? Can any thought be expressed with more economy? Is anything pompous or pretentious or faddish? Are you hanging on to something useless just because you think it's beautiful?

Simplify, simplify.

4. Style

So much for early warnings about the bloated monsters that lie in ambush for the writer trying to put together a clean English sentence.

"But," you may say, "if I eliminate everything that you think is clutter and strip every sentence to its barest bones, will there be anything left of me?"

The question is a fair one and the fear entirely natural. Simplicity carried to its extreme might seem to point to a style where the sentences are little more sophisticated than "Dick likes Jane" and "See Spot run."

I'll answer the question first on the level of mere carpentry. Then I'll get to the larger issue of who the writer is and how to preserve his or her identity.

Few people realize how badly they write. Nobody has shown them how much excess or murkiness has crept into their style and how it obstructs what they are trying to say. If you give me an article that runs to eight pages and I tell you to cut it to four, you'll howl and say it can't be done. Then you will go home and do it, and it will be infinitely better. After that comes the hard part: cutting it to three.

The point is that you have to strip down your writing before you can build it back up. You must know what the essential tools are and what job they were designed to do. If I may labor the metaphor of carpentry, it is first necessary to be able to saw wood neatly and to drive nails. Later you can bevel the edges or add elegant finials, if that is your taste. But you can never forget that you are practicing a craft that is based on certain principles. If the nails are weak, your house will collapse. If your verbs are weak and your syntax is rickety, your sentences will fall apart.

I'll admit that various nonfiction writers like Tom Wolfe and Norman Mailer and Hunter Thompson have built some remarkable houses. But these are writers who spent years learning their craft, and when at last they raised their fanciful turrets and hanging gardens, to the surprise of all of us who never dreamed of such ornamentation, they knew what they were doing. Nobody becomes Tom Wolfe overnight, not even Tom Wolfe.

First, then, learn to hammer in the nails, and if what you build is sturdy and serviceable, take satisfaction in its plain strength.

But you will be impatient to find a "style"—to embellish the plain words so that readers will recognize you as someone special. You will reach for gaudy similes and tinseled adjectives, as if "style" were something you could buy at a style store and drape onto your words in bright decorator colors. (Decorator colors are the colors that decorators come in.) Resist this shopping expedition: there is no style store.

Style is organic to the person doing the writing, as much a part of him as his hair, or, if he is bald, his lack of it. Trying to add style is like adding a toupee. At first glance the formerly bald man looks young and even handsome. But at second glance —and with a toupee there is always a second glance—he doesn't look quite right. The problem is not that he doesn't look well groomed; he does, and we can only admire the wigmaker's almost perfect skill. The point is that he doesn't look like himself.

This is the problem of the writer who sets out deliberately to garnish his prose. You lose whatever it is that makes you unique. The reader will usually notice if you are putting on airs. He wants the person who is talking to him to sound genuine. Therefore a fundamental rule is: be yourself.

No rule, however, is harder to follow. It requires the writer to do two things which by his metabolism are impossible. He must relax and he must have confidence.

Telling a writer to relax is like telling a man to relax while being prodded for a possible hernia, and, as for confidence, he is a bundle of anxieties. See how stiffly he sits at his typewriter, glaring at the paper that awaits his words, chewing the eraser on the pencil that is so sharp because he has sharpened it so many times. A writer will do anything to avoid the act of writing. I can testify from my newspaper days that the number of trips made to the water cooler per reporter-hour far exceeds the body's known need for fluids.

What can be done to put the writer out of these miseries? Unfortunately, no cure has yet been found. I can only offer the consoling thought that you are not alone. Some days will go better than others; some will go so badly that you will despair of ever writing again. We have all had many of these days and will have many more.

Still, it would be nice to keep the bad days to a minimum, which brings me back to the matter of trying to relax.

As I said earlier, the average writer sets out to commit an act of literature. He thinks that his article must be of a certain length or it won't seem important. He thinks how august it will look in print. He thinks of all the people who will read it. He thinks that it must have the solid weight of authority. He thinks that its style must dazzle. No wonder he tightens: he is so busy thinking of his awesome responsibility to the finished article that he can't even start. Yet he vows to be worthy of the task. He will do it—by God!—and, casting about for heavy phrases that would never occur to him if he weren't trying so hard to make an impression, he plunges in.

Paragraph 1 is a disaster—a tissue of ponderous generalities that seem to have come out of a machine. No *person* could have written them. Paragraph 2 is not much better. But Paragraph 3 begins to have a somewhat human quality, and by Paragraph 4 the writer begins to sound like himself. He has started to relax.

It is amazing how often an editor can simply throw away the first three or four paragraphs of an article and start with the paragraph where the writer begins to sound like himself. Not only are the first few paragraphs hopelessly impersonal and ornate; they also don't really say anything. They are a self-conscious attempt at a fancy introduction, and none is necessary.

A writer is obviously at his most natural and relaxed when he writes in the first person. Writing is, after all, a personal transaction between two people, even if it is conducted on paper, and the transaction will go well to the extent that it retains its humanity. Therefore I almost always urge people to write in the first person—to use "I" and "me" and "we" and "us." They usually put up a fight.

"Who am I to say what *I* think?" they ask. "Or what *I* feel?"

"Who are you *not* to say what you think?" I reply. "There's only one you. Nobody else thinks or feels in exactly the same way."

"But no one cares about my opinions," they say. "It would make me feel conspicuous."

"They'll care if you tell them something interesting," I say, "and tell them in words that come naturally."

Nevertheless, getting writers to use "I" is seldom easy. They think they must somehow earn the right to reveal their emotions or their deepest thoughts. Or that it is egotistical. Or that it is undignified—a fear that hobbles the academic world. Hence the professorial use of "one" ("One finds oneself not wholly in accord with Dr. Maltby's view of the human condition") and of the impersonal "it is" ("It is to be hoped that Professor Felt's essay will find the wider audience that it most assuredly deserves"). These are arid constructions. "One" is a pedantic fellow—I've never wanted to meet him. I want a professor with a passion for his subject to tell me why it fascinates *him.*

I realize that there are vast regions of writing where "I" is not allowed. Newspapers don't want "I" in their news stories; many magazines don't want it in their articles and features; businesses and institutions don't want it in the annual reports and pamphlets that they send so profusely into the American home. Colleges don't want "I" in their term papers or dissertations, and English teachers in elementary and high schools have been taught to discourage any first-person pronoun except the literary "we" ("We see in Melville's symbolic use of the white whale . . .").

Many of these prohibitions are valid. Newspaper articles should consist of news, reported as objectively as possible. And I sympathize with schoolteachers who don't want to give students an easy escape into opinion—"I think Hamlet was stupid" —before the students have grappled with the discipline of assessing a work on its merits and on external sources. "I" can be a self-indulgence and a cop-out.

Still, we have become a society fearful of revealing who we are. We have evolved a national language of impersonality. The institutions that seek our support by sending us their brochures tend to sound remarkably alike, though surely all of them— hospitals, schools, libraries, museums—were founded and are still sustained by men and women with different dreams and visions. Where are these people? It is hard to glimpse them among all the passive sentences that say "initiatives were undertaken" and "priorities have been identified."

Even when "I" is not permitted, it's still possible to convey a sense of I-ness. James Reston and Red Smith, for instance, don't use "I" in their columns; yet I have a good idea of what kind of people they are, and I could say the same of other essayists and reporters. Good writers are always visible just be-

hind their words. If you aren't allowed to use "I," at least think
"I" while you write, or write the first draft in the first person
and then take the "I"s out. It will warm up your impersonal
style.

Style, of course, is ultimately tied to the psyche, and writing
has deep psychological roots. The reasons why we express ourselves as we do, or fail to express ourselves because of "writer's
block," are buried partly in the subconscious mind. There are
as many different kinds of writer's block as there are kinds of
writers, and I have no intention of trying to untangle them
here. This is a short book, and my name isn't Sigmund Freud.

But I'm struck by what seems to be a new reason for avoiding
"I" that runs even deeper than what is not allowed or what is
undignified. Americans are suddenly uncertain of what they
think and unwilling to go out on a limb—an odd turn of events
for a nation famous for the "rugged individualist." A generation
ago our leaders told us where they stood and what they believed. Today they perform the most strenuous verbal feats to
escape this fate. Watch them wriggle through *Meet the Press* or
Face the Nation without committing themselves on a single
issue.

President Ford, trying to assure a group of visiting businessmen that his fiscal policies would work, said: "We see nothing
but increasingly brighter clouds every month." I took this to
mean that the clouds were still fairly dark. Ford's sentence,
however, was just misty enough to say nothing and still sedate
his constituents.

But the true champ is Elliot Richardson, who held four major
Cabinet positions in the 1970s—Attorney General and Secretary
of Defense, Commerce and H.E.W. It's hard to know even
where to begin picking from his vast trove of equivocal state-
ments, but consider this one: "And yet, on balance, affirmative
action has, I think, been a qualified success." A thirteen-word
sentence with five hedging words. I give it first prize as the most
wishy-washy sentence of the decade, though a close rival would

be Richardson's analysis of how to ease boredom among assembly-line workers: "And so, at last, I come to the one firm conviction that I mentioned at the beginning: it is that the subject is too new for final judgments."

That's a firm conviction? Leaders who bob and weave like aging boxers don't inspire confidence—or deserve it. The same thing is true of writers. Sell yourself, and your subject will exert its own appeal. Believe in your own identity and your own opinions. Proceed with confidence, generating it, if necessary, by pure willpower. Writing is an act of ego and you might as well admit it. Use its energy to keep yourself going.

5. The Audience

Soon after you confront this matter of preserving your identity, another question will occur to you: "Who am I writing for?"

It is a fundamental question and it has a fundamental answer: you are writing for yourself. Don't try to visualize the great mass audience. There is no such audience—every reader is a different person. Don't try to guess what sort of thing editors might want to publish or what you think the country is in a mood to read. Editors and readers don't know what they want to read until they read it. Besides, they're always looking for something new.

Don't worry about whether the reader will "get it" if you indulge a sudden impulse for humor or nonsense. If it amuses you in the act of writing, put it in. (It can always be taken out later, but only you can put it in.) You are writing primarily to entertain yourself, and if you go about it with confidence you will also entertain the readers who are worth writing for. If you lose the dullards back in the dust, that's where they belong.

I realize that I have raised what may seem to be a paradox. Earlier I warned that the reader is an impatient bird, perched on the thin edge of distraction or sleep. Now I am saying that you must write for yourself and not be gnawed by constant worry over whether he is tagging along behind.

I'm talking about two different problems. One is craft, the other is attitude. The first is a question of mastering a precise skill; the second is a question of how you use that skill to express your personality.

In terms of craft, there is no excuse for losing the reader through sloppy workmanship. If he drowses off in the middle of your article because you have been careless about a technical detail, the fault is entirely yours. But on the larger issue of whether the reader likes you, or likes what you are saying, or how you are saying it, or agrees with it, or feels an affinity for your sense of humor or your vision of life, don't give him a moment's worry. You are who you are, he is who he is, and either you will get along or you won't.

Perhaps this still seems like a paradox—or at least an impossible mental act to perform. How can you think carefully about not losing the reader and still be so carefree about his opinion that you will be yourself? I can only assure you that they are two distinct processes.

First, work hard to master the tools. Simplify, prune and strive for order. Think of this as a mechanical act and soon your sentences will become cleaner. The act will never become as mechanical as, say, shaving or shampooing—you will always have to think about the various ways in which the tools can be used. But at least your sentences will be grounded in solid principles, and your chances of losing the reader will be smaller.

Think of the other process as a creative act—the expressing of who you are. Relax and say what you want to say. And since style is who you are, you only need to be true to yourself to find it gradually emerging from under the accumulated clutter and debris, growing more distinctive every day. Perhaps the style won't solidify for several years as *your* style, *your* voice—and, in fact, it shouldn't. Just as it takes time to find yourself as a person, it takes time to find yourself as a stylist, and even then, inevitably, your style will change as you grow older.

But whatever your age, be yourself when you write. Many old

men still write with the zest that they had in their twenties or
early thirties; obviously their ideas are still young. Other old
writers ramble and repeat themselves; their style is the tip-off
that they have turned into redundant bores. Many college students write as if they were desiccated alumni thirty years out.

Let's look at a few writers to see the sheer pleasure with
which they put onto paper their passions and their crotchets,
not caring whether the reader shares them or not. The first
excerpt is from "The Hen (An Appreciation)," written by E. B.
White in 1944, at the height of World War II:

> Chickens do not always enjoy an honorable position
> among city-bred people, although the egg, I notice, goes on
> and on. Right now the hen is in favor. The war has deified
> her and she is the darling of the home front, feted at confer-
> ence tables, praised in every smoking car, her girlish ways
> and curious habits the topic of many an excited husbandry-
> man to whom yesterday she was a stranger without honor
> or allure.
>
> My own attachment to the hen dates from 1907, and I
> have been faithful to her in good times and bad. Ours has
> not always been an easy relationship to maintain. At first,
> as a boy in a carefully zoned suburb, I had neighbors and
> police to reckon with; my chickens had to be as closely
> guarded as an underground newspaper. Later, as a man in
> the country, I had my old friends in town to reckon with,
> most of whom regarded the hen as a comic prop straight
> out of vaudeville. . . . Their scorn only increased my devo-
> tion to the hen. I remained loyal, as a man would to a bride
> whom his family received with open ridicule. Now it is my
> turn to wear the smile, as I listen to the enthusiastic cack-
> ling of urbanites, who have suddenly taken up the hen
> socially and who fill the air with their newfound ecstasy and
> knowledge and the relative charms of the New Hampshire
> Red and the Laced Wyandotte. You would think, from

their nervous cries of wonder and praise, that the hen was
hatched yesterday in the suburbs of New York, instead of
in the remote past in the jungles of India.

To a man who keeps hens, all poultry lore is exciting and
endlessly fascinating. Every spring I settle down with my
farm journal and read, with the same glazed expression on
my face, the age-old story of how to prepare a brooder
house. . . .

Now, there's a man writing about a subject that I have absolutely no interest in. Yet I enjoy this piece thoroughly. I like the
simple beauty of its style. I like the rhythms, the unexpected but
refreshing words ("deified," "allure," "cackling"), the specific
details like the Laced Wyandotte and the brooder house. But
mainly what I like is that this is a man telling me unabashedly
about a love affair with poultry that goes back to 1907. It is
written with humanity and warmth, and after three paragraphs
I know quite a lot about what sort of man this hen-lover is.

Or take a writer who is almost White's opposite in terms of
style, who relishes the opulent word for its very opulence and
does not deify the simple sentence. Yet they are brothers in
holding firm opinions and saying what they think. This is H. L.
Mencken reporting on the "Monkey Trial"—the trial of John
Scopes, the young teacher who taught the theory of evolution
in his Tennessee classroom—in the summer of 1925:

It was hot weather when they tried the infidel Scopes at
Dayton, Tenn., but I went down there very willingly, for
I was eager to see something of evangelical Christianity as
a going concern. In the big cities of the Republic, despite
the endless efforts of consecrated men, it is laid up with a
wasting disease. The very Sunday-school superintendents,
taking jazz from the stealthy radio, shake their fire-proof
legs; their pupils, moving into adolescence, no longer respond to the proliferating hormones by enlisting for mis-
sionary service in Africa, but resort to necking instead.

Even in Dayton, I found, though the mob was up to do
execution on Scopes, there was a strong smell of antinomi-
anism. The nine churches of the village were all half empty
on Sunday, and weeds choked their yards. Only two or
three of the resident pastors managed to sustain themselves by their ghostly science; the rest had to take orders
for mail-order pantaloons or work in the adjacent straw-
berry fields; one, I heard, was a barber. . . . Exactly twelve
minutes after I reached the village I was taken in tow by
a Christian man and introduced to the favorite tipple of the
Cumberland Range; half corn liquor and half Coca-Cola. It
seemed a dreadful dose to me, but I found that the Dayton
illuminati got it down with gusto, rubbing their tummies
and rolling their eyes. They were all hot for Genesis, but
their faces were too florid to belong to teetotalers, and
when a pretty girl came tripping down the main street,
they reached for the places where their neckties should
have been with all the amorous enterprise of movie stars.
. . .

This is pure Mencken, both in its surging momentum and in
its irreverence. At almost any page where you open one of his
books he is saying something sure to outrage the professed
pieties of his countrymen. The sanctity in which Americans
bathed their heroes, their churches and their edifying laws—
especially Prohibition—was a well of hypocrisy for him that
never even came close to drying up. Some of his heaviest am-
munition he hurled at Presidents and politicians—his portrait of
"The Archangel Woodrow" still scorches the pages after half a
century—and as for Christian believers and clerical folk in general, they turn up unfailingly as mountebanks and boobs.

It may seem a miracle that Mencken could get away with
such heresies in the 1920s, when hero worship was an American
religion and the self-righteous wrath of the Bible Belt oozed
from coast to coast. In fact, not only did he get away with it; he

was the most revered and influential journalist of his generation. The impact that he made on subsequent writers of nonfiction is beyond measuring, and even now his topical pieces seem as fresh as if they were written yesterday.

The secret of his popularity—aside from his pyrotechnical use of the American language—was that he was obviously writing for himself and didn't worry over what the reader might think. It wasn't necessary to share his prejudices to enjoy seeing them expressed with such mirthful abandon. Mencken was never timid or evasive. He didn't kowtow to the reader or curry his favor. It takes courage to be such a writer, but it is out of such courage that revered and influential journalists are born.

Lest I seem to be choosing my writers only from the safe and distant past, let me close with two examples from the early 1970s. One is a shot straight into the veins from *Fear and Loathing in Las Vegas,* by Hunter S. Thompson. We find our author stopping by the roadside in his drive across Nevada to cover the National District Attorneys' Conference on Narcotics and Dangerous Drugs. The irony of this particular reporter assigned to this particular conference is rich enough to out-Mencken Mencken. If Thompson has consumed only a fraction of the stuff that he claims to swallow, his brain must be pure watermelon.

Luckily, nobody bothered me while I ran a quick inventory on the kit-bag. The stash was a hopeless mess, all churned together and half-crushed. Some of the mescaline pellets had disintegrated into a reddish-brown powder, but I counted about 35 or 40 still intact. My attorney had eaten all the reds, but there was quite a bit of speed left . . . no more grass, the coke bottle was empty, one acid blotter, a nice brown lump of opium hash and six loose amyls . . . Not enough for anything serious, but a careful rationing of mescaline would probably get us through the four-day Drug Conference.

On the outskirts of Vegas I stopped at a neighborhood

pharmacy and bought two quarts of Gold tequila, two fifths
of Chivas Regal and a pint of ether. I was tempted to ask
for some amyls. My angina pectoris was starting to act up.
But the druggist had the eyes of a mean Baptist hysteric.
I told him I needed the ether to get the tape off my legs,
but by that time he'd already rung the stuff up and bagged
it.

I wondered what he would say if I asked him for $22
worth of Romilar and a tank of nitrous oxide. Probably he
would have sold it to me. Why not? Free enterprise . . . give
the public what it needs—especially this bad-sweaty, ner-
vous-talkin' fella with tape all over his legs and this terrible
cough, along with angina pectoris and these godawful
aneuristic flashes every time he gets in the sun. I mean, this
fella was in bad shape, officer. How the hell was I to know
he'd walk straight out to his car and start abusing those
drugs?

Well, there's a man writing for himself and not looking over
his shoulder to see if the reader is clucking his tongue. Whether
he is writing the exact truth—or has raised it a few notches to
make a point about hypocrisy and greed in modern America—
is not the point. The point is that he is writing well, and with
humor, an acidhead-Mencken reincarnated for the 1970s.

My other example is from *How to Survive in Your Native
Land*, a book by James Herndon describing his experiences as
a teacher in a California junior high school. Of all the earnest
books on this subject which sprouted in America a decade ago,
Herndon's is—for me—the one that best captures how it really
was. His style is not quite like anybody else's, but his voice is
absolutely true. Here's how the book starts:

I might as well begin with Piston. Piston was, as a matter
of description, a red-headed medium-sized chubby eighth-
grader; his definitive characteristic was, however, stub-
bornness. Without going into a lot of detail, it became clear

right away that what Piston didn't want to do, Piston didn't
do; what Piston wanted to do, Piston did.

It really wasn't much of a problem. Piston wanted mainly
to paint, draw monsters, scratch designs on mimeograph
blanks and print them up, write an occasional horror story
—some kids referred to him as The Ghoul—and when he
didn't want to do any of those, he wanted to roam the halls
and on occasion (we heard) investigate the girls' bathrooms.

We had minor confrontations. Once I wanted everyone
to sit down and listen to what I had to say—something
about the way they had been acting in the halls. I was
letting them come and go freely and it was up to them (I
planned to point out) not to raise hell so that I had to hear
about it from other teachers. Sitting down was the issue—
I was determined everyone was going to do it first, then I'd
talk. Piston remained standing. I re-ordered. He paid no
attention. I pointed out that I was talking to him. He in-
dicated he heard me. I inquired then why in hell didn't he
sit down. He said he didn't want to. I said I did want him
to. He said that didn't matter to him. I said do it anyway.
He said why? I said because I said so. He said he wouldn't.
I said Look I want you to sit down and listen to what I'm
going to say. He said he *was* listening. I'll listen but I won't
sit down.

Well, that's the way it goes sometimes in schools. You as
teacher become obsessed with an issue—I was the injured
party, conferring, as usual, unheard-of freedoms, and here
they were as usual taking advantage. It ain't pleasant coming in the teachers' room for coffee and having to hear
somebody say that so-and-so and so-and-so from *your* class
were out in the halls *without a pass* and *making faces* and
giving the finger to kids in *my* class during the most *important* part of *my* lesson about *Egypt*—and you ought to be
allowed your tendentious speech, and most everyone will
allow it, sit down for it, but occasionally someone wises you

up by refusing to submit where it isn't necessary. . . . How did any of us get into this? we ought to be asking ourselves.

Any writer who uses "ain't" and "tendentious" in the same sentence, who quotes without using quotation marks, knows what he is doing. This seemingly artless style, so full of art, is ideal for Herndon's purpose. It avoids the pretentiousness that infects so much writing by people who are doing worthy work, and it allows for a rich vein of humor, humanity and common sense. Herndon sounds like a good teacher and like a person whose company I would enjoy. But ultimately he is writing for himself: an audience of one.

"Who am I writing for?" The question that begins this chapter has irked some readers; they want me to say "Whom am I writing for?" But I just can't say it. It's not me. It's not even I.

6. Words

There is a kind of writing that might be called journalese, and it is the death of freshness in anybody's style. It is the common currency of newspapers and of magazines like *Time*—a mixture of cheap words, made-up words and clichés which have become so pervasive that a writer can hardly help using them automatically. You must fight these phrases off or you will sound like every hack who sits down at a typewriter. In fact, you will never make your mark as a writer unless you develop a respect for words and a curiosity about their shades of meaning that is almost obsessive. The English language is rich in strong and supple words. Take the time to root around and find the ones you want.

What is "journalese"? It is a quilt of instant words patched together out of other parts of speech. Adjectives are used as nouns ("greats," "notables"). Nouns are used as adjectives ("top officials," "health reasons") or extended into adjectives ("insightful"). Nouns are used as verbs ("to host"), or they are chopped off to form verbs ("enthuse," "emote"), or they are padded to form verbs ("beef up," "put teeth into").

This is a world where eminent people are "famed" and their associates are "staffers," where the future is always "upcoming" and someone is forever "firing off" a note. Nobody in *Time* has

merely sent a note or a memo or a telegram in years. Famed
Diplomat Henry Kissinger, who hosted foreign notables to beef
up the morale of top State Department staffers, sat down and
fired off a lot of notes. Notes that are fired off are always fired
in anger and from a sitting position.

Here, for example, is an article from a newsmagazine that is
hard to match for sheer fatigue:

> Last February, Plainclothes Patrolman Frank Serpico
> knocked at the door of a suspected Brooklyn heroin pusher.
> When the door opened a crack, Serpico shouldered his way
> in only to be met by a .22-cal. pistol slug crashing into his
> face. Somehow he survived, although there are still buzz-
> ing fragments in his head, causing dizziness and permanent
> deafness in his left ear. Almost as painful is the suspicion
> that he may well have been set up for the shooting by other
> policemen. For Serpico, 35, has been waging a lonely, four-
> year war against the routine and endemic corruption that
> he and others claim is rife in the New York City police
> department. His efforts are now sending shock waves
> through the ranks of New York's finest. . . . Though the
> impact of the commission's upcoming report has yet to be
> felt, Serpico has little hope that . . .

The upcoming report has yet to be felt because it is still
upcoming, and as for the "permanent deafness," it is still a little
early to tell. And what makes those buzzing fragments buzz? I
would have thought that by now only Serpico's head would be
buzzing.

But apart from these lazinesses of logic, what makes the story
so infinitely tired is the failure of the writer to reach for anything but the nearest cliché. "Shouldered his way," "only to be
met," "crashing into his face," "waging a lonely war," "corruption that is rife," "sending shock waves," "New York's finest"—
these dreary phrases constitute journalese at its worst and writing at its most banal. We know just what to expect. No surprise

awaits us in the form of a bizarre word, an oblique look. We are in the hands of a hack and we know it right away.

Don't let yourself get in this position. The only way to fight it is to care deeply about words. If you find yourself writing that someone recently "enjoyed" a spell of illness or that a business has been "enjoying" a slump, stop and think how much they really enjoyed it. Notice the decisions that other writers make in their choice of words and be finicky about the ones that you select from the vast supply. The race in writing is not to the swift but to the original.

Make a habit of reading what is being written today and what has been written before. But cultivate the best writers. Don't assume that because an article is in a newspaper or a magazine it must be good. Lazy editing is endemic to American newspapers, and writers who use clichés by reflex are likely to work for editors who have seen so many clichés that they no longer even recognize them as they go limping by.

Also get in the habit of using dictionaries. My favorite for handy use is *Webster's New Collegiate,* based on the Second Edition of *Webster's New International Dictionary,* though, like all word freaks, I own many bigger dictionaries which will reward me in their own fashion when I am on some more specialized search. (Careful writers, incidentally, cling to their copy of any Webster dictionary based on the superb Second Edition because the Third Edition is too permissive.)

If you have any doubt of what a word means, look it up. Learn its etymology and notice what curious branches its original root has put forth. See if it has any other meanings that you didn't know it had. Master the small gradations between words that seem to be synonyms. What is the difference between "cajole," "wheedle," "blandish" and "coax"? An excellent guide to these nuances is *Webster's Dictionary of Synonyms.*

And don't scorn that bulging grab bag, *Roget's Thesaurus.* It's easy to regard the book as hilarious. Look up "villain," for example, and you will be awash in such rascality as only a lexicographer could conjure back from centuries of iniquity, obliquity, depravity, knavery, profligacy, frailty, flagrancy, infamy, immorality, corruption, wickedness, wrongdoing, backsliding and sin. You will find rogues and wretches, ruffians and riffraff, miscreants and malefactors, reprobates and rapscallions, hooligans and hoodlums, scamps and scapegraces, scoundrels and scalawags, jezebels and jades. You will find adjectives to fit them all (foul and fiendish, devilish and diabolical), and adverbs, and verbs to describe how the wrongdoers do their wrong, and cross-references leading to still other thickets of venality and vice. Still, there is no better friend to have around to nudge the memory than Roget. It saves you the time of rummaging in your own memory—that network of overloaded grooves—to find the word that is right on the tip of your tongue, where it doesn't do you any good. The *Thesaurus* is to the writer what a rhyming dictionary is to the songwriter—a reminder of all the choices—and you should use it with gratitude. If, having found the scalawag and the scapegrace, you want to know how they differ, *then* go to the dictionary.

Also bear in mind, when you are choosing words and stringing them together, how they sound. This may seem absurd: readers read with their eyes. But actually they hear what they are reading—in their inner ear—far more than you realize. Therefore such matters as rhythm and alliteration are vital to every sentence. A typical example—maybe not the best, but undeniably the nearest—is the preceding paragraph. Obviously I enjoyed making a certain arrangement of my ruffians and riffraff, my hooligans and hoodlums, and the reader enjoyed it, too—far more than if I had given him a mere list. He enjoyed not only the arrangement but the effort to entertain him. He wasn't enjoying it, however, with his eyes. He was enjoying it mainly in his ear.

E. B. White makes the case cogently in *The Elements of Style* (the best book on writing that I know) when he suggests trying to rearrange any phrase that has survived for a century or two, such as Thomas Paine's "These are the times that try men's souls":

> Times like these try men's souls.
> How trying it is to live in these times!
> These are trying times for men's souls.
> Soulwise, these are trying times.

Paine's phrase is like poetry and the other four are like oatmeal, which, of course, is the divine mystery of the creative process. Yet the good writer of prose must be part poet, always listening to what he writes. E. B. White continues across the years to be my favorite stylist because I am so conscious of being with a man who cares in his bones about the cadences and sonorities of the language. I relish (in my ear) the pattern that his words make as they fall into a sentence. I try to surmise how in rewriting the sentence he reassembled it to end with a phrase that will momentarily linger, or how he chose one word over another because he was after a certain emotional weight. It is the difference between, say, "serene" and "tranquil"—one so soft, the other strangely disturbing because of the unusual "n" and "q."

Such considerations of sound and rhythm should be woven through every aspect of what you write. If all your sentences move at the same plodding gait, which even you recognize as deadly but don't know how to cure, read them aloud. You will begin to hear where the trouble lies. See if you can gain variety by reversing the order of a sentence, by substituting a word that has freshness or oddity, by altering the length of your sentences so that they don't all sound as if they came out of the same computer. An occasional short sentence can carry a tremendous punch. It stays in the reader's ear.

Remember, then, that words are the only tools that you will be given. Learn to use them with originality and care. Value them for their strength and their infinite diversity. And also remember: somebody out there is listening.

7. Usage

All this talk about good words and bad words brings us to a gray but important area called "usage." What is good usage? What is good English? What newly minted words is it O.K. to use, and who is to be the judge? Is it O.K. to use "O.K."?

Earlier I mentioned an incident of college students hassling the administration, and in the last chapter I described myself as a word freak. Here are two typical specimens that have crept into the language in the past decade. "Hassle" is both a verb and a noun, meaning to give somebody a hard time, or the act of being given a hard time, and anyone who has ever been hassled by a petty bureaucrat for not properly filling out Form 35–BT will agree that it sounds exactly right. "Freak" in this new usage means an enthusiast, and there is no missing the aura of obsession that goes with calling somebody a jazz freak, or a chess freak, or a sun freak, though it would probably be pushing my luck to describe a man who compulsively visits circus sideshows as a freak freak.

Anyway, I accept both of these new arrivals wholeheartedly. I don't consider them slang, or put quotation marks around them to show that I'm mucking about in the argot of the youth culture and really know better. They're good words and we need them to express what they express. But I still won't accept "notables" and "greats" and "upcoming" and countless other newcomers. They are cheap words and we *don't* need them.

Why is one word good and another word cheap? I can't give you an answer because usage has no fixed boundaries or rules. Language is a fabric that changes from one week to another, adding new strands and dropping old ones, and even word freaks fight over what is allowable, often reaching their decision on a wholly subjective basis such as taste ("notables" is sleazy). Which still leaves the question of who our tastemakers are.

The question was confronted by the editors of a brand-new dictionary, *The American Heritage Dictionary*, at the outset of their task in the mid-1960s. They assembled a "Usage Panel" to help them appraise the new words and dubious constructions that had come knocking at the door. Which should be ushered in, which thrown out on their ear? The panel consisted of 104 men and women—mostly writers, poets, editors and teachers—who were known for caring about the language and trying to use it well.

I was a member of the panel, and over the next few years I kept getting questionnaires. Would I accept "finalize" and "escalate"? How did I feel about "It's me"? Would I allow "like" to be used as a conjunction—like so many people do? How about "mighty," as in "mighty fine"?

We were told that in the dictionary our opinions would be tabulated in a separate "Usage Note" so that readers could tell how we voted. The questionnaire also left room for any comments that we might feel impelled to make—a chance that the panelists seized avidly, as we found when the dictionary was published in 1969 and our comments were released to the press. Not surprisingly, our passions ran high.

"Good God, no! Never!" cried Barbara W. Tuchman, asked about the verb "to author." Scholarship hath no fury like that of a language purist faced with sludge, and I share Mrs. Tuchman's vow that "author" should never be authorized, just as I agree with Lewis Mumford that the adverb "good" should be

"left as the exclusive property of Ernest Hemingway" and with
Gerald Carson that "normalcy" should be "permitted only to
admirers of the late Warren G. Harding."

But guardians of usage are only doing half their job if they
merely keep the language from becoming sloppy. Any oaf can
rule that the suffix "wise," as in "mediawise," is oafwise, or that
being "rather unique" is no more possible than being rather
pregnant. The other half of the job is to help the language grow
by welcoming any immigrant that will bring strength or color.

Therefore I was glad to see that 97 percent of us voted to
admit "dropout," which is clean and vivid, but that only 47
percent would accept "senior citizen," which is pretentious
and patronizing, typical of the pudgy new intruders from
the land of sociology, where a janitor is a maintenance engineer. I'm glad we accepted "escalate," the kind of verbal
contraption which I generally dislike but which the Vietnam
war gave a precise meaning, complete with overtones of
blunder.

I'm glad we took into full membership all sorts of robust
words that previous dictionaries had derided as "colloquial":
adjectives like "rambunctious," verbs like "stall" and "trigger"
and "rile," nouns like "shambles" and "tycoon" and "trek," the
latter approved by 78 percent to mean any difficult trip, as in
"the commuter's daily trek to Manhattan." Originally it was a
Cape Dutch word applied to the Boers' arduous journey by ox
wagon. But our panel evidently felt that the Manhattan commuter's daily trek is no less arduous.

Still, 22 percent of us were unwilling to let "trek" slip into
general usage. This was the virtue of revealing how our panel
voted—it put our agreements and our discords on display, and
now a writer who is in doubt can conduct himself accordingly.
Thus our 95 percent vote against "myself," as in "He invited
Mary and myself to dinner," a word condemned as "prissy,"
"horrible" and "a genteelism," ought to warn off anyone who
doesn't want to be prissy, horrible and genteel. As Red Smith

put it, " 'Myself' is the refuge of idiots taught early that 'me' is a dirty word."

On the other hand, only 66 percent of our panel rejected the verb "to contact," and only half opposed the split infinitive and the verbs "to fault" and "to bus." So only 50 percent of your readers will fault you if you decide to voluntarily call your school board and to bus your children to another town. If you contact your school board you risk your reputation by another 16 percent. Our apparent rule of thumb was stated by Theodore M. Bernstein: "We should apply the test of convenience. Does the word fill a real need? If it does, let's give it a franchise." I agree with Bernstein. "Hassle," for instance, seems to me to fill a real need.

All of this merely confirms what lexicographers have always known: that the laws of usage are relative, bending with the taste of the lawmaker. One of our panelists, Katherine Anne Porter, called "O.K." a "detestable vulgarity" and claimed that she has never spoken the word in her life, whereas I freely admit that I have spoken the word "O.K." "Most," as in "most everyone," was scorned as "cute farmer talk" by Isaac Asimov and embraced as a "good English idiom" by Virgil Thomson.

"Regime," meaning any administration, as in "the Truman regime," drew the approval of most everyone on the panel, as did "dynasty." But they drew the wrath of Jacques Barzun, who said, "These are technical terms, you blasted non-historians!" Probably I gave my O.K. to "regime" when I filled out the questionnaire. Now, chided by Barzun for imprecision, I think it looks like journalese. One of the words that *I* railed against was "personality," as in a "TV personality." But now I wonder if it isn't the only word for that vast swarm of people who are famous for being famous—and, possibly, for nothing else. What, for instance, do the Gabor sisters really *do?*

In the end it comes down to one question: What is "correct" usage? We have no king to establish the King's English; we only have the President's English—which we don't want. Webster,

long a defender of the faith, muddied the waters in 1961 with
its permissive Third Edition, which argued that almost anything goes as long as somebody uses it, noting that "ain't" is
"used orally in most parts of the U.S. by many cultivated speakers."

Just where Webster cultivated those speakers I ain't sure.
Nevertheless it's true that the spoken language is looser than
the written language, and *The American Heritage Dictionary*
properly put its question to us in both forms. Often we allowed
an oral idiom which we forbade in print as too informal, fully
realizing, however, that "the pen must at length comply with
the tongue," as Samuel Johnson said, and that today's spoken
garbage may be tomorrow's written gold. Certainly the growing acceptance of the split infinitive, or of the preposition at the
end of a sentence, proves that formal syntax can't hold the fort
forever against a speaker's more comfortable way of getting the
same thing said. A sentence is a fine thing to put a preposition
at the end of. As for "It's me," who would defend to the death
"It is I"? Only a purity freak.

Our panel recognized that correctness can even vary within
a particular word. We voted heavily against "cohort," for instance, as a synonym for "colleague," except where the tone
was jocular. Thus a professor would not be among his cohorts
at a faculty meeting, but they would abound at his college
reunion, wearing funny hats. We rejected "too" as a synonym
for "very," as in "His health is not too good." Whose health is?
But we approved it in wry or humorous use, as in "He was not
too happy when she ignored him."

These may seem like picayune distinctions. They're not. They
are signals to the reader that you are sensitive to the many
shadings of usage. "Too," when substituted for "very," is clutter
—"He didn't feel too much like going shopping"—and should
be cut out. But the wry example in the previous paragraph is
worthy of Ring Lardner. It adds a tinge of sarcasm that wouldn't
otherwise be there.

Did any pattern emerge from the opinions of our panel when we finally ended our task, or were we just flexing our prejudices and pedantries? Luckily, a pattern did emerge, and it offers a guideline that is still useful. In general we turned out to be liberal in accepting new words and phrases, but conservative in grammar.

It would be foolish, for instance, to reject a word as perfect as "dropout," or to pretend that countless words are not entering the gates of correct usage every day, borne on the winds of science and technology, fad and fashion, social change and social concern: "moonscape," "meltdown," "printout," "unisex," "afro," "pantyhose," "skyjacker," "feminism," "consumerism," "wetlands," "biodegradable," "sexist," "lib," "macho," "uptight," "paraprofessional" and hundreds more.

It would also be foolish not to at least consider all the wonderfully short words invented by the counterculture in the 1960s as a way of lashing back at the bloated verbiage of the Establishment: "bag," "scene," "trip," "rap," "crash," "trash," "fuzz," "funky," "split," "rip-off," "vibes," "downer," "bummer," et al. If brevity is a prize, these were sure winners.

The only trouble with accepting words that entered the language overnight is that they have a tendency to leave as abruptly as they came. The "happenings" of the late 1960s no longer happen, "out of sight" is out of sight, nobody does his "thing" anymore, "relevant" has been hooted out of the room, and where only yesterday we wanted our leaders to have "charisma," or at least "clout," today we want them to be "together." Be vigilant, therefore, about instant change. The writer who cares about usage must always know the quick from the dead.

As for the area where our Usage Panel was conservative, we strictly upheld most of the classic distinctions in grammar—"can" and "may," "fewer" and "less," "eldest" and "oldest," etc.—and decried the classic errors, insisting that "flout" still doesn't mean "flaunt," no matter how many writers flaunt their ignorance by flouting the rule, and that "fortuitous" still means "accidental," "disinterested" still means "impartial," and "infer" doesn't mean "imply."

Here we were motivated by our love of the language's beautiful precision. We hate to see our favorite tools mistreated. As Dwight Macdonald put it, "Simple illiteracy is no basis for linguistic evolution." This is where correct usage will win or lose you the readers you would most like to win. Know the difference between a "reference" and an "allusion," between "connive" and "conspire," between "compare with" and "compare to." If you must use "comprise," use it right.

"I choose always the grammatical form unless it sounds affected," explained Marianne Moore, and that finally is where our usage panel took its stand. We were not pedants, so hung up on correctness that we didn't want the language to keep refreshing itself with phrases like "hung up." But that didn't mean we had to accept every atrocity that has come stumbling in, like "hopefully."

Prayerfully these examples will help you to approach the question of "What is good usage?" but fearfully you will sometimes slide off the track. And if that sentence doesn't explain why "hopefully" is bad usage, go back to "Go."

Meanwhile the battle continues. Several years ago the Usage Panel was reconstituted, with new members added, and we continue to receive ballots soliciting our opinion on new words and locutions: verbs like "definitize" ("Congress definitized a proposal") and "attrit" ("to attrit the population base of the enemy"), nouns like "affordables" and "collectibles," colloquialisms like "the bottom line" and "up front," and strays like "into" ("he's into backgammon and she's into jogging").

Fortunately, it no longer takes a panel of experts to notice that jargon is inundating many areas of American life, especially government, business, education and the social sciences. President Carter signed an executive order directing that federal regulations be written "simply and clearly"; corporations and law firms have hired consultants to make their prose less murky and specialized, and even the insurance industry is trying to rewrite its policies to tell us in less disastrous English what redress will be ours when disaster strikes.

Whether these efforts will do much good I wouldn't want to bet, nor, probably, would Jimmy the Greek. Still there is comfort in the sight of so many people standing Canute-like on the beach, aware of the danger and trying to hold back the tide. That's where all careful writers ought to be, looking at every new piece of debris that washes up and asking "Do we need it?"

I remember the first time somebody asked me—only a few years ago—"How does that impact you?" I had always thought that "impact" was a noun, except in dentistry, which I try not to think of at all. Then I began to meet "de-impact," usually in connection with programs to de-impact the effects of a hard winter or some other adversity. Nouns now turn overnight into verbs. We target goals and we access facts. My train conductor announces that the train won't platform in Darien.

I see that Detroit is downsizing its cars but still hoping to attract upscale customers. (Small Cadillacs for rich people.) It's part of an ongoing effort to save energy. All efforts in America today are "ongoing." So are all programs and investigations. So, in fact, are all people and all forms of life; when we cease to be ongoing we are dead. "Ongoing" is a jargon word that is wholly unnecessary except to raise morale. We face our daily job with more zest if the boss reminds us that it's an ongoing project; we give more willingly to institutions if they have targeted our funds for ongoing improvements.

One hospital wrote me about its plan to "modernize, expand and reconfigure" its facilities. When did "reconfigure" poke its haughty nose into our ongoing life? We were all doing fine without it. I would certainly hope that any architect trying to modernize a facility would move things around in response to new needs. "Reconfigure" gives his work the necessary grandeur to raise the necessary cash. Otherwise a donor might fall prey to "disincentivization."

I could go on. I have enough horrible examples to fill a book, but it's not a book that I would want anyone to read. We are still left with the question: What is good usage? Perhaps one helpful new way of looking at the question is to try to separate usage from jargon.

I would say, for instance, that "prioritize" is jargon—a pompous new verb that sounds more important than "rank"—and that "bottom line" is usage, a metaphor borrowed from the world of bookkeeping which conveys an image that we can picture. As every businessman knows, the bottom line is the one that ultimately matters. It tells how things stand after all the gains and losses have been toted up. If someone says, "The bottom line is that we just can't work together," we know what he means. I don't particularly like the phrase, but the bottom line is that it's probably here to stay.

New usages also arrive with new political events. Just as Vietnam gave us "escalate," Watergate gave us a whole lexicon of words connoting obstruction and deceit, such as "stonewall," "deep-six" and "launder." It is a fitting irony that under Richard Nixon "launder" became a dirty word. Today when we hear that someone laundered his funds in Mexico to hide the origin of the money and the route that it took, the word has a precise meaning. It's short, it's vivid, and we need it. I accept "launder" and "stonewall"; I don't accept "prioritize" and "disincentive."

I would suggest a similar guideline for separating good English from technical English. It's the difference between, say, "printout" and "input." A printout is a specific object that a computer emits when it is asked for information. Before the advent of computers it wasn't needed. Now it is. But it has stayed where it belongs—in the world where computers are used. Not so with "input," which was invented to describe the information that is fed to a computer. The word has broken out of the machine and run wild. Our input is sought on every

\

subject, from diets and pets to philosophical discourse ("I'd like your input on whether God really exists").

I don't want to give somebody my input and get his feedback, though I'd be glad to offer my ideas. To me, good usage consists of using good words if they already exist—as they usually do—to express myself clearly and simply to someone else. You might say it's how I try to verbalize the interpersonal.

PART II

8. Unity

You learn to write by writing. It is a truism worn thin by repetition, but it is still true, and it can't be repeated often enough. The only way to learn to write is to force yourself to produce a certain number of words on a regular basis.

If you went to work for a newspaper which required you to write two or three articles every day, you would be a better writer after six months. You wouldn't necessarily be writing well—your style might still be pedestrian, full of clutter and clichés. But at least you would be exercising your powers of putting the English language on paper, gaining confidence, and identifying the commonest problems.

All writing is ultimately a question of solving a problem. It may be a problem of where to obtain the facts, or how to organize the material. It may be a problem of approach or attitude, tone or style. Whatever it is, it has to be confronted and solved.

Sometimes you will despair of finding the right solution—or any solution. You will think: "If I live to be ninety I'll never get out of this mess I'm in." I have often thought it myself. But when I finally do solve the problem it's because I have written millions and millions of words. Like a surgeon doing his five hundredth appendix operation, I've been there before and

have a surer instinct than the beginner about how to fix what
has gone wrong.

So now I'll put you to actual writing. First I wanted to give
you a set of attitudes and broader principles. Now the task is to
apply these principles to the various forms that nonfiction can
take: the interview, the travel piece, the science article, sports,
criticism, humor and all the hybrid species that can result from
mixing them together. Every form has its special pitfalls. But all
of them share one horrible problem: how to get started. No
element of writing causes so much anguish as "the lead," and
with almost no further ado I will try to wrestle it into partial
submission. The only ado that I will first commit is to suggest
that before you struggle with the lead you make certain decisions about what tone you want to adopt. Get your unities
straight.

Unity is the anchor of good writing. It not only keeps the
reader from straggling off in all directions; it satisfies his subconscious need for order and assures him that all is well at the
helm. Therefore choose from among the many variables and
stick to your choice.

One choice is unity of pronoun. Are you going to write in the
first person as a participant or in the third person as an observer? Or even in the second person, that darling of sportswriters hung up on Hemingway ("You knew this had to be the most
spine-tingling clash of giants you'd ever seen from a pressbox
seat, and you weren't just some green kid who was still wet
behind the ears")?

Unity of tense is another choice. Most people write mainly in
the past tense ("I went up to Boston the other day"), but some
people write agreeably in the present ("I'm sitting in the dining
car of the Yankee Limited and we're pulling into Boston").
What is not agreeable is to switch back and forth. I'm not saying
that you can't use more than one tense. Obviously the whole
purpose of tenses is to enable a writer to deal with time in its
various gradations from the past to the hypothetical future

("When I telephoned my girl from the Boston station I realized that if I had written to tell her I would be coming she would have waited for me"). What I am saying is that you must choose the tense in which you are *principally* going to address the reader, no matter how many glances you may take backward or forward along the way.

Another choice is unity of mood. You might want to talk to the reader in the casual and chatty voice that *The New Yorker* has so strenuously refined. Or you might want to approach him with a certain formality to describe a serious event or to acquaint him with a set of important facts. Both tones are acceptable; in fact, *any* tone is acceptable. But don't mix two or three.

Such fatal mixtures are common in the nonfiction of writers who haven't yet learned control. Travel writing is a conspicuous case. "My wife, Ann, and I had always wanted to visit Hong Kong," the writer begins, his blood astir with reminiscence, "and one day last spring we found ourselves looking at an airline poster and I said, 'Let's go!' The kids were grown up or in school," he continues, and proceeds to describe in genial detail how they stopped off in Hawaii and had such a comical time changing their money at the Hong Kong airport and finding their hotel. Fine. He is a real person taking us along on a real trip, and we can identify with him and Ann.

Suddenly he turns into a travel brochure. "Hong Kong affords many fascinating experiences to the curious sightseer," he writes. "One can ride the picturesque ferry from Kowloon and gawk at the myriad sampans as they scuttle across the teeming harbor, or take a day's trip to browse in the alleys of fabled Macao with its colorful history as a den of smuggling and intrigue. You will want to take the quaint funicular that climbs . . ." Then we get back to him and Ann and their efforts to eat at Chinese restaurants, and again all is well. Everyone is interested in food and we are being told about a personal quest.

Then suddenly the writer is a guidebook: "To enter Hong Kong it is necessary to have a valid passport but no visa is required. You should definitely be immunized against smallpox and you would also be well advised to consult your physician with regard to a possible inoculation for typhoid. The climate in Hong Kong is seasonable except in July and August when . . ." Our writer is gone, and so is Ann, and so—very soon—are we.

It is not that the scuttling sampans and the smallpox shots should not be included. What annoys us is that the writer never decided what kind of article he wanted to write or how he wanted to approach us. He comes at us in many guises, depending on what kind of material he is trying to purvey. Instead of controlling his material, his material is controlling him. This wouldn't happen if he took time to establish certain unities.

Therefore ask yourself some basic questions before you start. For example: "In what capacity am I going to address the reader?" (Reporter? Provider of information? Average man or woman?) "What pronoun and tense am I going to use?" "What style?" (Impersonal reportorial? Personal but formal? Personal and casual?) "What attitude am I going to take toward the material?" (Involved? Detached? Judgmental? Ironic? Amused?) "How much do I want to cover?" "What one point do I really want to make?"

The last two questions are more important than they might seem. Most nonfiction writers have a definitiveness complex. They feel that their article must be the last word and the most comprehensive word. It's a commendable impulse, but there is no definitive article. What you think is definitive today will turn undefinitive by tomorrow, and the writer who doggedly pursues every last fact will find himself pursuing the rainbow and never settling down to write. Decide what corner of your subject you are going to bite off, and be content to cover it well and stop. You can always come back another day and bite off another corner.

As for what point you want to make, I'll state as a useful rule of thumb that every successful piece of nonfiction should leave the reader with one provocative thought that he didn't have before. Not two thoughts, or five—just one. So try to decide what point you most want to leave in the reader's mind. It will not only give you a better idea of what route you ought to follow and what destination you hope to reach; it will also affect your decision about tone and attitude. Some points are best made by dry understatement, some by heavy irony.

Once you have these unities decided, there is no material that you can't work into your frame. If the man writing about Hong Kong had chosen to write solely in the conversational vein about what he and Ann thought and did, he would have found a natural way to weave into his narrative whatever he wanted to tell us about the Kowloon ferry and the local weather. His personality and purpose would be intact, and his article would hold together.

Now, it's possible that you will make these prior decisions and then discover that they were not the right ones. The material seems to be leading you in an unexpected direction where you are more comfortable writing in a different tone. This is not abnormal—the very act of writing will often summon out of the brain some cluster of thoughts or memories which you didn't anticipate.

Don't fight such a current if it feels right. Trust your material if it is taking you into terrain that you didn't intend to enter but where the vibrations are good. Adjust your style and your mood accordingly and proceed to whatever destination you reach. Don't ever become the prisoner of a preconceived plan. Writing is no respecter of blueprints—it is too subjective a process, too full of surprises.

Of course if this happens, the second part of your article will be badly out of joint with the first. But at least you will know which part is truest to your instincts. Then it is just a matter of making repairs. Go back to the beginning and rewrite it so that the mood and style are consistent.

There is nothing in such a method to be ashamed of. Scissors

and paste are honorable writers' tools. Just remember that all
the unities must be fitted into the edifice that you finally put
together, however backwardly they may fall into place, or it will
soon come tumbling down.

9. The Lead

The most important sentence in any article is the first one. If it doesn't induce the reader to proceed to the second sentence, your article is dead. And if the second sentence doesn't induce him to continue to the third sentence, it is equally dead. Of such a progression of sentences, each tugging the reader forward until he is safely hooked, a writer constructs that fateful unit: the "lead."

How long should the lead be? One or two paragraphs? Four or five? There is no pat answer. Some leads hook the reader with just a few well-baited sentences; others amble on for several pages, exerting a slow but steady pull. Every article poses a different problem, and the only valid test is: Does it work? Your lead may not be the best of all possible leads, but if it does the job that it is supposed to do, be thankful and proceed.

Sometimes the length may depend on the audience that you are writing for. Readers of *The New Yorker* or of a literary review, for instance, expect the writer to start somewhat discursively, and they will stick with him for the pleasure of wondering where he will emerge as he moves in leisurely circles toward his eventual point. But I urge you not to count on the reader to stick around. He is a fidgety fellow who wants to know —very soon—what's in it for him.

Therefore the lead must capture the reader immediately and force him to keep reading. It must cajole him with freshness or novelty or paradox, or with humor, or with surprise, or with an unusual idea, or an interesting fact, or a question. Anything will do as long as it nudges his curiosity and tugs at his sleeve.

Next the lead must do some real work. It must provide a few hard details that tell the reader why the piece was written and why he ought to read it. But don't dwell on the reason. Coax the reader a little more; keep him inquisitive.

Continue to build. Every paragraph should amplify the one that preceded it. Give more thought to adding solid detail and less to entertaining the reader. But take special care with the last sentence of each paragraph—it is the crucial springboard to the next paragraph. Try to give that sentence an extra twist of humor or surprise, like the periodic "snapper" in the routine of a stand-up comic. Make the reader smile and you've got him for at least one paragraph more.

Let's look at a few leads that vary in pace but are alike in maintaining pressure. I'll start with three columns of my own that first appeared in, respectively, *Life, The Saturday Evening Post* and *Look*—three magazines which, judging by the comments of readers, found their consumers mainly in barbershops, hairdressing salons and airplanes ("I was getting a haircut the other day and I saw your article"). I mention this as a reminder that far more periodical reading is done in America under the dryer than under the reading lamp, so there isn't much time for the writer to fool around.

I don't claim that these are three best leads I could have found; I only know that they work. The first is the lead of a piece called "Block That Chickenfurter":

I've often wondered what goes into a hot dog. Now I know and I wish I didn't.

Two very short sentences. But it would be hard not to continue to the second paragraph:

My trouble began when the Department of Agriculture published the hot dog's ingredients—everything that may legally qualify—because it was asked by the poultry industry to relax the conditions under which the ingredients might also include chicken. In other words, can a chicken-furter find happiness in the land of the frank?

One sentence that explains the incident on which the column is based. Then a snapper to restore the easygoing tone.

Judging by the 1,066 mainly hostile answers that the Department got when it sent out a questionnaire on this point, the very thought is unthinkable. The public mood was most felicitously caught by the woman who replied: "I don't eat feather meat of no kind."

Another fact and another smile. Whenever you are lucky enough to unearth a quotation as funny as that, find a way to use it—preferably at the end of a paragraph.

The article then specifies what the Department of Agriculture says may go into a hot dog—a list that includes "the edible part of the muscle of cattle, sheep, swine or goats, in the diaphragm, in the heart or in the esophagus . . . [but not including] the muscle found in the lips, snout or ears."

From there it progresses—not without an involuntary reflex around the esophagus—into an account of the controversy between the poultry interests and the frankfurter interests, which in turn leads to the point that Americans will eat anything that even remotely resembles a hot dog. Implicit at the end is the larger point that Americans don't know, or care, what goes into the food they eat. The style of the article has remained casual and touched with humor throughout. But its content turns out to be more serious than the reader expected when he was drawn into it by a somewhat whimsical lead.

Here's another lead, from an article that was called "Does He or Doesn't He?":

Until this year I have always wanted to smell as good as
the next man. But now the next man wants to smell too
good. The boom in male cosmetics is sweeping America at
such speed—sales went over half a billion dollars in 1965
alone and are growing fast—that one of the country's most
popular entertainers recently refused to tell the name of
the scent that he was wearing. Too many other men, he
explained, would also start to wear it.

That entertainer's secret would be safe with me. He
could tell me the name of his scent tomorrow and I swear
I wouldn't call up my pharmacy. Nor do I own a single face
cream, and I've never been to any of the men's "hair sty-
lists" for a tinting or a spray. I go to a funny old-fashioned
barber who just cuts my hair and doesn't try to make me
look younger than when I went in. If anything, his conversation sends me out older.

The last sentence does no real work—it's a tiny joke and not a
very good one. But it propels the reader on to the third paragraph, where the article gets down to business:

All of this makes me a member of America's newest
minority group: an adult male untouched by rejuvenating
lotions, fragrances and dyes. "A case of galloping vanity has
hit men in this country," Eugenia Sheppard writes, "and
any minute now there'll be masks, moisturizers, home hair
coloring and hair sprays for men."

That minute is almost here. Hardly a day goes by when
I don't read in the paper or see in a TV commercial some
new evidence that . . .

The article goes on to document the growing American belief
that a man who looks young and glossy is more competent than
his visibly aging colleague. From there it veers off, in a turn just
sharp enough to catch the reader off balance, to arrive at the
sober point which it intended all along to reach—that this is a

crazy way for a society to operate. In style the unities continue to be intact: "I don't want to touch—or retouch—a hair of the gray heads that ponder my financial, legal and medical affairs. . . . I like to think that every one of their gray hairs was honorably earned, every facial line etched by a mistake that they will not make again." But the substance is far deeper than the reader anticipated when he was being pampered through the first few paragraphs. What remains with him is not the lead, but the point.

A slightly slower lead, luring the reader more with curiosity than with humor, introduced a piece called "Thank God for Nuts":

> By any reasonable standard, nobody would want to look twice—or even once—at the piece of slippery elm bark from Clear Lake, Wisc., birthplace of pitcher Burleigh Grimes, that is on display at the National Baseball Museum and Hall of Fame in Cooperstown, N.Y. As the label explains, it is the kind of bark that Grimes chewed during games "to increase saliva for throwing the spitball. When wet, the ball sailed to the plate in deceptive fashion." This would seem to be one of the least interesting facts available in America today.
>
> But baseball fans can't be judged by any reasonable standard. We are obsessed by the minutiae of the game and nagged for the rest of our lives by the memory of players we once saw play. No item is therefore too trivial which puts us back in touch with them. I am just old enough to remember Burleigh Grimes and his well-moistened pitches sailing deceptively to the plate, and when I found his bark I studied it as intently as if I had come upon the Rosetta Stone. "So *that's* how he did it," I thought, peering at the odd botanical relic. "Slippery elm! I'll be damned."
>
> This was only one of several hundred encounters that I had with my own boyhood as I prowled through the Mu-

seum, a handsome brick building on Main Street, only a
peanut bag's throw from the pasture where Abner Doubleday allegedly invented the game in 1839. Probably no other
museum is so personal a pilgrimage to our past . . .

The reader is now safely hooked, and the hardest part of the
writer's job is over.

One reason for citing this lead is to point out that salvation
often lies not in the writer's style but in some odd fact that he
was able to discover. I remember that I went up to Coopers-
town and spent a whole afternoon in the museum, taking volu-
minous notes. Jostled everywhere by nostalgia, I gazed with
reverence at Lou Gehrig's locker and Bobby Thomson's game-
winning bat; I sat in a grandstand seat brought from the Polo
Grounds, dug my unspiked soles into the home plate from Eb-
bets Field, and dutifully copied all the labels and captions that
might be useful.

"These are the shoes that touched home plate as Ted
finished his journey around the bases," said the label identifying the shoes worn by Ted Williams when he hit a home run
on his last time at bat. The shoes were in much better shape
than the pair—rotted open at the sides—that belonged to Walter Johnson. But again the caption provided exactly the kind
of justifying fact that a baseball nut would want. "My feet
must be comfortable when I'm out there a-pitching," the
great Walter said.

The museum closed at five and I returned to my motel secure
in my memories and in my research. But instinct told me to go
back the next morning for a final tour, and it was only then that
I noticed Burleigh Grimes' slippery elm bark, which struck me
as an ideal lead. It still does.

One moral of this story is that you should always collect more
material than you will eventually use. Every article is strong in
proportion to the surplus of details from which you can choose
the few that will serve you best—if you don't go on gathering

facts forever. At some point you must decide to stop researching and start writing.

An even more important moral is to look for your material everywhere, not just by reading the obvious sources and interviewing the obvious people. Look at signs and at billboards and at all the junk written along the American roadside. Read the labels on our packages and the instructions on our toys, the claims on our medicines and the graffiti on our walls.

Read the fillers, so rich in self-esteem, that come spilling out of your monthly statement from the electric company and the telephone company and the bank. Read menus and catalogues and second-class mail. Nose about in obscure crannies of the newspaper, like the Sunday real estate section—you can tell the temper of a society by what patio accessories it wants. Our daily landscape is thick with absurd messages and portents. Notice them. They not only have a certain social significance; they are often just quirky enough to make a lead that is different from everybody else's.

And speaking of everybody else's lead, there are several categories that I'd be glad never to see again. One is the future archeologist: "When some future archeologist stumbles upon the remains of our civilization a thousand years from now, what will he make of the jukebox?" I'm tired of him already and he's not even here. I'm also tired of the visitor from Mars: "If a creature from Mars landed on our planet tomorrow, he would be amazed to see hordes of scantily clad earthlings lying on the sand and barbecuing their skins." And I'm tired of the cute event that just happened to happen "one day not long ago" or on a conveniently recent Saturday afternoon. "One day not long ago a small button-nosed boy was walking with his dog, Terry, in a field outside Paramus, N.J., when he saw something that looked strangely like a balloon rising out of the ground." Let's retire the future archeologist and the man from Mars and the button-nosed boy. Try to give your lead a freshness of perception or detail.

Consider this lead, by Joan Didion, on a piece called "7000 Romaine, Los Angeles 38":

Seven Thousand Romaine Street is in that part of Los Angeles familiar to admirers of Raymond Chandler and Dashiell Hammett: the underside of Hollywood, south of Sunset Boulevard, a middle-class slum of "model studios" and warehouses and two-family bungalows. Because Paramount and Columbia and Desilu and the Samuel Goldwyn studios are nearby, many of the people who live around here have some tenuous connection with the motion-picture industry. They once processed fan photographs, say, or knew Jean Harlow's manicurist. 7000 Romaine looks itself like a faded movie exterior, a pastel building with chipped *art moderne* detailing, the windows now either boarded or paned with chicken-wire glass and, at the entrance, among the dusty oleander, a rubber mat that reads WELCOME.

Actually no one is welcome, for 7000 Romaine belongs to Howard Hughes, and the door is locked. That the Hughes "communications center" should lie here in the dull sunlight of Hammett-Chandler country is one of those circumstances that satisfy one's suspicion that life is indeed a scenario, for the Hughes empire has been in our time the only industrial complex in the world—involving, over the years, machinery manufacture, foreign oil-tool subsidiaries, a brewery, two airlines, immense real-estate holdings, a major motion-picture studio, and an electronics and missile operation—run by a man whose *modus operandi* most closely resembles that of a character in *The Big Sleep*.

As it happens, I live not far from 7000 Romaine, and I make a point of driving past it every now and then, I suppose in the same spirit that Arthurian scholars visit the Cornish coast. I am interested in the folklore of Howard Hughes . . .

What is pulling us into this article—toward, we hope, some glimpse of how Hughes operates, some hint of the riddle of the Sphinx—is the steady accretion of facts that have pathos and faded glamour. Knowing Jean Harlow's manicurist is such a minimal link to glory, the unwelcoming welcome mat such a queer relic of a golden age when Hollywood's windows weren't paned with chicken-wire glass and the roost was ruled by giants like Mayer and De Mille and Zanuck who could actually be seen alive and exercising their mighty power. We want to know more; we read on.

Another writer whose leads I admire is Garry Wills. Almost every chapter in his *Nixon Agonistes,* for instance, which originated as a series of magazine articles, begins with an arrangement of sentences that dazzle me with their gathering momentum and mordant truth:

Spiro Agnew's career has about it a somnambulistic sure-footedness, an inevitability of advance, that reminds one of Mencken's Coolidge, of the juggernaut of snooze. In an election-eve TV broadcast, Hubert Humphrey proudly displayed Ed Muskie, his monkish second-string Eugene McCarthy. Nixon, on the same night, sat alone, remasticating answers for Bud Wilkinson, his kept TV interrogator. No Agnew in sight. It was said that Nixon regretted his choice, his deal with Thurmond. But Agnew was a guided missile, swung into place, aimed, activated, launched with the minute calculation that marks Nixon. Once the missile was fired, the less attention it drew to itself the better—like a torpedo churning quiet toward its goal. Agnew has a neckless, lidded flow to him, with wraparound hair, a tubular perfection to his suits or golf outfits, quiet burbling oratory. Subaquatic. He was almost out of sight by campaign's end; but a good sonar system could hear him burrowing ahead, on course.

It's a fine lead, doing its job with precise detail, unexpected imagery and words as surprising as a rare bird. Wills is holding his reader in a tight grip but never patronizing him.

I also admire the leads of Paul O'Neil, whose articles in *Life* adorned that magazine for many years with elegance and wit. What I like is the sense of enjoyment that O'Neil always brings to his subject. He never forgets that a successful writer must also be to some extent an entertainer. Most aspiring writers don't like to think of themselves as entertainers—the word is beneath their dignity. That's why they remain aspiring writers and don't become Paul O'Neil.

Here's one of his typical leads.

A real eater is hard to find. Oh, any baseball player can do one-sitting bulk work—seven steaks, 83 hot dogs, two bushels of blue points—particularly if the goods are free. But we're talking about the sort of fellow you can send into restaurants to do undercover jobs. Gourmets are no good —too picky, too quarrelsome and, like other dilettantes, alas, too apt to break down under steady pounding. Your man needs a knowledge of wines and a memory for sauces, but he must digest well too, and be ready to unfold a napkin again after only a short nap. Above all, he must have a cool head, a hard eye and judgment born of professional experience. You have to go to France to find the genuine article. Even in France, if you want a big leaguer, you must choose among only eight men—all employed by the *Guide Michelin,* which has been rating French restaurants for 62 years.

A few weeks ago, happily, *Life* was able to borrow Michelin inspector Pierre Lamalle for a fortnight, fly him to New York and set him to eating his way around the United States. His American colleagues in the project were, it must be confessed, startled on inspecting him for the first time. It was impossible not to wonder, as did the New York fight mob on inspecting Georges Carpentier a few decades before, whether the champion of France was not just an overrated middleweight after all. Pierre was not only disconcertingly young (29) but alarmingly flat in the belly.

And yet there can be no fixed rules for how to write a lead. Within the broad principle of not letting the reader get away, every writer must approach his subject in a manner that most naturally suits what he is writing about and who he is. In proof of which, I'll close with the lead of an article on rugby written by Richard Burton, the actor. Its second sentence is one of the longest I've ever seen, but it is under control all the way. Besides, it sounds very Welsh, and if that's how Welshmen talk it's how they ought to write:

> It's difficult for me to know where to start with rugby. I come from a fanatically rugby-conscious Welsh miner's family, know so much about it, have read so much about it, have heard with delight so many massive lies and stupendous exaggerations about it and have contributed my own fair share, and five of my six brothers played it, one with some distinction, and I mean I even knew a Welsh woman from Taibach who before a home match at Aberavon would drop goals from around 40 yards with either foot to entertain the crowd, and her name, I remember, was Annie Mort and she wore sturdy shoes, the kind one reads about in books as "sensible," though the recipient of a kick from one of Annie's shoes would have been not so much sensible as insensible, and I even knew a chap called Five-Cush Cannon who won the sixth replay of a cup final (the previous five encounters having ended with the scores 0–0, 0–0, 0–0, 0–0, 0–0, including extra time) by throwing the ball over the bar from a scrum 10 yards out in a deep fog and claiming a dropped goal. And getting it.

10. The Ending

After so many words suggesting how to get started, I should add a few on how to stop. Knowing when to end an article is far more important than most writers realize. In fact, you should give as much thought to choosing your last sentence as you did to your first. Well, almost as much.

This may seem ridiculous. If the reader has stuck with you from the beginning, trailing you around blind corners and over bumpy terrain, surely he won't leave when the end is in sight. But he will—because the end that is in sight often turns out to be a mirage. Like the minister's sermon that builds to a series of perfect conclusions which never conclude, an article that doesn't stop at its proper stopping place is suddenly a drag and therefore, ultimately, a failure.

We are most of us still prisoners of the lesson pounded into us by the composition teachers of our youth: that every story must have a beginning, a middle and an end. We can still visualize the outline, with its Roman numerals (I, II and III), which staked out the road that we would faithfully trudge, and its sub-numerals (IIa and IIb) denoting lesser paths down which we would briefly poke. But we always promised to get back to III and summarize our journey.

This is all right for elementary and high school students uncertain of their ground. It forces them to see that every piece of writing should have a logical design which introduces and develops a theme. It's a lesson worth knowing at any age—even the professional writer is adrift more often than he would like to admit. But if you are going to write good nonfiction, you must wriggle out of III's dread grip.

You will know you have arrived at III when you see emerging from your typewriter a sentence that begins, "In sum, therefore, it can be noted that . . ." Or a question that asks, "What insights, then, have we been able to glean from . . . ?" These are signals to the reader that you are about to repeat in compressed form what you have already told him in detail. His interest begins to falter; the tension that you have built begins to sag.

Yet you will be true to Miss Potter, your teacher, who made you swear eternal fealty to the holy outline. You remind the reader of what can, in sum, therefore, be noted. You go gleaning one more time in insights that you have already adduced.

But the reader hears the laborious sound of cranking. He sees what you are doing and how bored you are by it. He feels the stirrings of resentment. Why didn't you give more thought to how you were going to wind this thing up? Or are you summarizing because you think he was too dumb to get the point? Still, you keep cranking. But the reader has another option. He quits.

This is the negative reason for realizing the importance of the last sentence. Failure to know where that sentence should occur—and what it should consist of—can wreck an article which until its final stage has been tightly constructed.

The positive reason for ending well is not just to avoid ending badly, but because a good last sentence—or paragraph—is a joy in itself. It has its own virtues which give the reader a lift and which linger when the article is over.

The perfect ending should take the reader slightly by surprise and yet seem exactly right to him. He didn't expect the article to end so soon, or so abruptly, or to say what it said. But he knows it when he sees it. Like a good lead, it works. It is like the curtain line in a theatrical comedy. We are in the middle of a scene (we think) when suddenly one of the actors says something funny, or outrageous, or epigrammatic, and the lights go out. We are momentarily startled to find the scene over, and then delighted by the aptness of how it ended. What delights us, subconsciously, is the playwright's perfect control.

For the nonfiction writer, the simplest way of putting this into a rule is: when you're ready to stop, stop. If you have presented all the facts and made the point that you want to make, look for the nearest exit.

Often it takes just a few sentences to get out of the article in the same style that you used to get in. Going back to Garry Wills' *Nixon Agonistes*, here is how he ends the chapter on "Ted" Agnew, whom we last saw launched missile-like, sub-aquatic, into the political ocean of American life:

> There is a difference between ambition and opportun-
> ism. Leisurely "Ted" is not driven by Nixon's demons. He
> does not knock himself out; he does not even do his home-
> work. But he is opportunistic—not cynically so; when lucky
> breaks come, one takes them, grateful. Man's function is to
> reap the fruits of our beneficent system. How foolish of "the
> kids" not to understand this. As he told them in the cam-
> paign: "You may give us your symptoms; we will make the
> diagnosis and we, the Establishment, will implement the
> cure." It is a message that he did not try to take to Miami's
> blacks.

The blunt irony of that final sentence brings echoes of Mencken rumbling down the decades again, as so often hap-pens for me when one of America's bleakest truths is seen through a glass plainly. Here is how Mencken ends his appraisal of Coolidge, whose appeal to the "customers" was that his "gov-ernment governed hardly at all; thus the ideal of Jefferson was realized at last, and the Jeffersonians were delighted":

We suffer most, not when the White House is a peaceful
dormitory, but when it [has] a tin-pot Paul bawling from
the roof. Counting out Harding as a cipher only, Dr. Coolidge was preceded by one World Saver and followed by
two more. What enlightened American, having to choose
between any of them and another Coolidge, would hesitate
for an instant? There were no thrills while he reigned, but
neither were there any headaches. He had no ideas, and he
was not a nuisance.

These are the elements to look for when instinct tells you that
it's time to stop. Both the Agnew sentence and the Coolidge
sentence send the reader on his way quickly and with a provocative thought to take along. The notion of Coolidge having no
ideas and not being a nuisance is bound to leave a residue of
enjoyment. It works.

But what often works best is a quotation. Try to find in your
notes some remark which has a sense of finality, or which is
funny, or which adds an unexpected last detail. Sometimes it
will jump out at you in the process of writing. Put it aside and
save it. If the remark doesn't jump out, go back and look for it
among all the things said or written by anyone mentioned in the
article.

In the mid-1960s, when Woody Allen was just becoming established as the nation's resident neurotic, still mainly doing
nightclub monologues, I wrote the first long magazine piece
that took note of his arrival. It ended like this:

"If people come away relating to me as a person," Allen
says, "rather than just enjoying my jokes; if they come away
wanting to hear me again, no matter what I might talk
about, then I'm succeeding." Judging by the returns, he is.
Woody Allen is Mr. Related-To, Mr. Pop Therapy, and he
seems a good bet to hold the franchise for many years.

Yet he does have a problem all his own, unshared by,
unrelated to, the rest of America. "I'm obsessed," he says,

"by the fact that my mother genuinely resembles Groucho Marx."

There's a remark from so far out in left field that nobody could see it coming. The surprise that it carries is tremendous. How could it not be a perfect ending?

Surprise is one of the most refreshing commodities in nonfiction and, as I'll try to demonstrate next, there is nothing like human detail to make a story come alive.

11. The Interview

Get people talking. Learn to ask questions that will elicit answers about what is most interesting or vivid in their lives. Nothing so animates writing as someone telling what he thinks or what he does—in his own words.

His own words will always be better than your words, even if you are the most elegant stylist in the land. They carry the inflection of his speaking voice and the idiosyncrasies of how he puts a sentence together. They contain the regionalisms of his conversation and the lingo of his trade. They convey his enthusiasms. This is a person talking to the reader directly, not through the filter of a writer. As soon as a writer steps in, everybody else's experience becomes secondhand.

Therefore learn how to conduct an interview. Whatever form of nonfiction you write, it will come alive in proportion to the number of "quotes" that you can weave into it naturally as you go along. Often, in fact, you will find yourself embarking on an article so apparently lifeless—the history of an institution, perhaps, or some local issue such as storm sewers—that you will quail at the prospect of keeping your readers, or even yourself, awake.

Take heart. You will find the solution if you look for the human element. Somewhere in every drab institution are men

and women who have a fierce attachment to what they are
doing and are rich repositories of lore. Somewhere behind
every storm sewer is a politician whose future hangs on getting
it installed and a widow who has always lived on the block and
is outraged that some damn-fool legislator thinks it will wash
away. Find these people to tell your story and it won't be drab.

I have proved this to myself many times. In 1961 I undertook
to write a small book for The New York Public Library to cele-
brate the fiftieth anniversary of its main building on Fifth Avenue. On the surface it seemed to be just the story of a marble
building and millions of musty volumes. But behind the façade
I found that the Library had nineteen research divisions, each
with a curator supervising a hoard of treasures and oddities,
from Washington's handwritten Farewell Address to 750,000
movie stills. I decided to interview all these curators to learn
what was in their collections, what they were adding to keep up
with new areas of knowledge and how their rooms were being
used.

I found, for instance, that the Science and Technology division had a collection of patents second only to that of the United
States Patent Office and was therefore almost a second home to
the city's patent lawyers. But it also had a daily stream of men
and women who obviously thought they were on the verge of
discovering perpetual motion. "Everybody's got something to
invent," the curator explained, "but they won't tell us what
they're looking for—maybe because they think we'll patent it
ourselves."

The whole building turned out to be just such a mixture of
scholars and searchers and crackpots, and my story, though
ostensibly the chronicle of an institution, was really a story
about people.

I used the same approach in a long article about Sotheby's,
the thriving London auction firm. Sotheby's was also divided
into various domains, such as silver and porcelain and art, each
with an expert in charge, and, like the Library, it subsisted on

the whims of a capricious public. The experts were like department heads in a small college, and all of them had anecdotes that were unique both in substance and in the manner of telling:

"We just sit here like Micawber waiting for things to come in," said R. S. Timewell, head of the furniture department. "Recently an old lady near Cambridge wrote that she wanted to raise two thousand pounds and asked if I would go through her house and see if her furniture would fetch that much. I did, and there was absolutely nothing of value. As I was about to leave I said, 'Have I seen *every* thing?' She said I had, except for a maid's room that she hadn't bothered to show me. The room had a very fine 18th-century chest that the old lady was using to store blankets in. 'Your worries are over,' I told her, 'if you sell that chest.' She said, 'But that's quite impossible—where will I store my blankets?' "

My worries were over, too. By listening to the quizzical scholars who ran the business and to the men and women who flocked there every morning bearing unloved objects found in British attics ("I'm afraid it *isn't* Queen Anne, Madam—much nearer Queen Victoria, unfortunately") I got as much human detail as a writer could want.

Finally, when I was asked in 1966 to write a history of the Book-of-the-Month Club to mark its fortieth birthday and 200-millionth book, I thought I might encounter nothing but inert matter. But again I found a peppery human element on both sides of the fence, for the books have always been selected by a panel of strong-minded judges and sent to equally stubborn subscribers, who never hesitated to wrap up a book that they didn't like and to send it right back.

I was given more than 1,000 pages of transcribed interviews with the five original judges (Heywood Broun, Henry Seidel Canby, Dorothy Canfield, Christopher Morley and William

Allen White), to which I added my own interviews with the
Club's founder, Harry Scherman, and with the judges who were
then active (John Mason Brown, Clifton Fadiman, Gilbert High-
et and John K. Hutchens). The result was four decades' worth
of personal memories on how America's reading tastes had
changed, and why, and even the books took on a life of their
own and became characters in my story:

> "Probably it's difficult for anyone who remembers the
> prodigious success of Gone With the Wind," Dorothy Can-
> field said, "to think how it would have seemed to people
> who encountered it simply as a very, very long and detailed
> book about the Civil War and its aftermath. We had never
> heard of the author and didn't have anybody else's opinion
> on it. It was chosen with a little difficulty, because some of
> the characterization was not very authentic or convincing.
> But as a narrative it had the quality which the French call
> *attention:* it made you want to turn over the page to see
> what happens next. I remember that someone com-
> mented, 'Well, people may not like it very much, but no-
> body can deny that it gives a lot of reading for your money.'
> Its tremendous success was, I must say, about as surprising
> to us as to anybody else."

These three examples are typical of the kind of information
that is locked inside people's heads which a good nonfiction
writer must unlock. The best way to practice is to go out and
interview people. The interview itself is one of the most common and popular nonfiction forms, so you might as well master
it early.

   How should you start? First, decide what person you want to
interview. If you are a college student, don't interview your
roommate. With all due respect for what a fine fellow he is, he
probably doesn't have much to say that the rest of us want to
hear. To learn the craft of nonfiction you must push yourself out
into the real world—your town or your city or your county—

and pretend that you are writing for a real publication. If it helps, decide which publication you are hypothetically writing for. In any case, choose as your subject someone whose job is so important, or interesting, or unusual, that the average reader would want to read about him.

This doesn't mean that he has to be president of General Motors. He can be the owner of the local pizza parlor or super-market or hairdressing academy. He can be the fisherman who puts out every morning, or the Little League manager, or the cop. He can be the butcher, the baker or—better yet, if you can find him—the candlestick maker. Look for the women in your community who are unraveling the old myths about what the two sexes were foreordained to do. Choose, in short, someone who touches some corner of the reader's life.

Interviewing is one of those skills that you can only get better at. You will never again feel so ill at ease as when you try it for the first time, and probably you will never feel entirely comfort-able prodding another person for answers that he or she may be too shy to reveal, or too inarticulate. But at least half of the skill is purely mechanical. The rest is instinct—knowing how to make the other person relax, when to push, when to listen, when to stop. And this can all be learned with experience.

The basic tools for an interview are paper and two or three well-sharpened pencils. Is that the most insultingly obvious ad-vice you have ever been given? You'd be surprised how many writers venture forth to stalk their quarry with no pencil, or with one that breaks, or with a pen that doesn't work, and with nothing to write on. "Be prepared" is as apt a motto for the nonfiction writer on his mundane rounds as it is for the Boy Scout alert for the traditional old lady trying to cross the street.

But keep your notebook or paper out of sight until you need it. There is nothing less likely to relax a person than the arrival of someone with a stenographer's pad. You both need time to get to know each other. Take a while just to chat, gauging what sort of person you are dealing with, getting him to trust you.

Never go into an interview without doing whatever home-
work you can. If you are interviewing a town official, know his
voting record. If it's an actor, know what plays he has been in.
You will be resented if you inquire about facts that you could
have learned in advance.

Make a list of likely questions—it will save you the vast em-
barrassment of going dry in mid-interview. Perhaps you won't
need it; better questions will occur to you, or the person being
interviewed will veer off at an angle that you couldn't have
foreseen. Here you can only go by intuition. If he strays hopelessly off the subject, drag him back. If you like the new direction, follow him and forget the questions that you intended to
ask.

Many beginning interviewers are crippled by the fear that
they are imposing on the other person and have no right to
invade his privacy. This fear is almost 100 percent unfounded.
Unless the other person is a Howard Hughes, he is delighted
that somebody wants to interview him. Most men and women
lead lives, if not of quiet desperation, at least of desperate quiet-
ness, and they jump at a chance to talk about their work to an
outsider who seems eager to listen.

This doesn't necessarily mean that it will go well. In general
you will be talking to people who have never been interviewed
before, and they will warm to the process awkwardly, self-
consciously, perhaps not giving you anything that you can use.
Come back another day; it will go better. You will both even
begin to enjoy it—proof that you aren't forcing your victim to
do something that he doesn't really want to do.

Speaking of tools, you will ask if it's all right to use a tape
recorder. Why not just take one along, start it going, and forget
all that business of pencil and paper?

Obviously the tape recorder is a superb instrument for cap-
turing what people have to say—especially people who, for
reasons of their culture or education or temperament, would
never get around to writing it down. I admire the books of Studs

Terkel, like *Hard Times: The Story of the Great Depression*, which he "wrote" by recording long interviews with ordinary people and stitching the results into coherent shape. I admire the oral histories of Spanish-speaking people similarly "written" by Oscar Lewis, such as *La Vida*. In this realm of social anthropology the tape recorder is literally invaluable. I also like the question-and-answer interviews, obtained by tape recorder, that have long been published in *Playboy* and *Rolling Stone*. They have the sound of spontaneity and the refreshing absence of a writer hovering over the product and burnishing it to a high gloss.

But, strictly, this isn't writing. It's a process of asking questions and then pruning and splicing the answers, and I can testify that it takes an infinitude of time and care and labor. People who seem to be talking into the tape recorder with linear precision and taut economy turn out, when the interview is transcribed, to have been stumbling so aimlessly over the sands of grammar that they have hardly completed a single decent sentence. Hence my admiration for Terkel and Lewis and other stewards of the spoken word. The seemingly simple use of a tape recorder isn't simple.

But my main reasons for warning you off it are practical and tangible. The practical hazards hardly need to be mentioned. One is that you don't usually have a tape recorder with you—you are more apt to have a pencil. Another is that tape recorders malfunction. Few moments in journalism are as glum as the return of a reporter with "a really great story," followed by his pushing of the Play button and total silence.

My tangible reason is that there should be a relationship between a writer and his materials, just as there should be a relationship between an artist and his canvas and his brush. The act of taking notes is, however fragmentary, an act of writing. To bypass this process by having someone talk into a machine is to lose the subtle mystery of seeing words emerge as you put them on paper.

This is especially important in an interview. Someone is telling you something; you are writing it down. It is a human
transaction that has been going on for thousands of years.

But there is a problem: he is talking faster than you can write.
You are still scribbling Sentence A when he zooms into Sentence B. You drop Sentence A and pursue him into Sentence B,
meanwhile trying to hold the rest of Sentence A in your inner
ear and hoping that Sentence C will be a dud that you can skip
altogether, using the time to catch up. Unfortunately, you now
have your man going at high speed. He is at last saying all the
things that you have been trying to cajole out of him for an hour,
and saying them with what seems to be Churchillian eloquence.
Your inner ear is clogging up with sentences that you want to
grab before they slip away.

Tell him to stop. Just say, "Hold it a minute, please," and
write until you catch up. What you are trying to do with your
feverish scribbling, after all, is to quote him correctly, and nobody wants to be misquoted.

With practice you will write faster and develop some form of
shorthand. You will find yourself devising abbreviations for oft-
en-used words and also omitting the small connective syntax. As
soon as the interview is over, fill in all the missing words that
you can remember. Complete the uncompleted sentences.
Most of them will still be lingering just within the bounds of
recall.

When you get home, type out your notes—now an almost
illegible scrawl—so that you can read them easily. This not only
makes the interview accessible, along with any clippings or
other materials that you may have assembled. It enables you to
review in tranquillity a torrent of words that you wrote in haste,
and thereby discover what the person really said.

You will find that he said much that is redundant or dull. Try
to single out the quotations that are most important or colorful.
You will be tempted to use all the words that are in your notes
because you performed the laborious chore of getting all the

words down. This is no reason for putting the reader to the same trouble. Your job is to distill the essence.

What about your obligation to the person you interviewed? To what extent can you cut or juggle his words? This question vexes every writer returning from his first interview—and it should. But the answer is not hard if you keep in mind two standards: brevity and fair play.

Your ethical duty to the person being interviewed is to present his position accurately. If he carefully weighed two sides of an issue and you only quote his views of one side, making him seem to favor that position, you will misrepresent what he told you. Or you might misrepresent him by quoting him out of context, or by choosing only some flashy remark without adding the serious afterthought. You are dealing with a man's honor and reputation—and also with your own.

But after that your duty is to the reader. He deserves the smallest package. Most people meander in their conversation, filling it with irrelevant tales and trivia. Much of it is delightful, but it is still trivia. Your interview will be strong to the extent that you get the main points made without waste.

Therefore if you find on page 5 of your notes a comment which perfectly amplifies a point on page 2—a point made earlier in the interview—you will do everyone a favor if you link the two thoughts, letting the second sentence follow and illustrate the first. This may violate the truth of how the interview progressed, but you will be true to the intent of what was said. Play with the "quotes" by all means—selecting, rejecting, thinning, transposing their order, saving a good one for the end. Just make sure that the play is fair. Don't change any words or let the cutting of a sentence distort the proper context of what remains.

This is really my case against the tape recorder. A writer should always be able to *see* his materials. If your interview is on tape you become a listener, forever fussing with the machine, running it backward to find a brilliant remark that you can't quite find, running it forward, stopping, starting, driving yourself crazy. Be a writer. Write things down.

As for how to organize the interview, every one is different, so I will leave you to discern its logical shape and will only add a few technical hints.

The lead obviously should tell the reader, like all leads, why the person is worth reading about. What is his claim to our time and attention?

Thereafter, try to achieve a balance between what the subject is saying in *his* words and what you are writing in *your* words to explain and to connect. If you quote a person for three or four consecutive paragraphs, this becomes monotonous. Quotations are livelier when you break them up, making periodic appearances in your role as guide. You are still the writer —don't relinquish control. But make your appearances useful; don't just insert one of those dreary sentences which shout to the reader that your sole purpose is to break up a string of quotations ("He stopped and tapped his pipe on a nearby ashtray and I noticed that his fingers were quite long").

When you use a quotation, start the sentence with it. Don't lead up to it with a vapid phrase saying what the man said.

GOOD: "I usually like to go downtown once a week," Mr. Smith said, "and have lunch with some of my old friends."

BAD: Mr. Smith said that he liked to "go downtown once a week and have lunch with some of my old friends."

The first sentence has vitality, the second is dead. In fact, nothing is deader than to start a sentence with a "Mr. Smith said" construction—it's where countless readers stop reading. If the man said it, let him say it and get the sentence off to a warm, human start.

But be careful where you break the quotation. Do it as soon as you naturally can, so that the reader knows who is talking, but not where it will destroy the rhythm or the sense. Notice how the following three variants all inflict some kind of damage:

"I usually like," Mr. Smith said, "to go downtown once a week and have lunch with some of my old friends."

"I usually like to go downtown," Mr. Smith said, "once a week and have lunch with some of my old friends."

"I usually like to go downtown once a week and have lunch," Mr. Smith said, "with some of my old friends."

Finally, don't strain to find synonyms for "he said." Don't make your man assert, aver and expostulate just to avoid repeating "he said," and please—please!—don't write "he smiled" or "he grinned." I have never heard anybody smile. The reader's eye skips over "he said" anyway, so it's not worth a lot of fuss. If you crave variety, choose synonyms that catch the shifting nature of the conversation. "He pointed out," "he explained," "he replied," "he added"—these all carry a particular meaning. But don't use "he added" if the man is merely averring and not putting a postscript on what he just said.

I'll close by adding as a postscript a passage from *The Bottom of the Harbor,* by Joseph Mitchell, my own favorite writer of long nonfiction articles and possibly America's best. The book consists of various articles that Mitchell wrote for *The New Yorker* about people who live and work around the waterfront. One reason I admire Joseph Mitchell is that he is a master of the uncommonly difficult art of writing about the so-called common man without ever patronizing him.

This is part of an interview with the captain of a fishing boat called a "dragger" that operates out of Stonington, Connecticut. Note the deceptively simple style, the exactness of detail and especially the deft interweaving of Mitchell's words with those of the captain, Ellery Thompson:

Ellery is a self-taught B-flat trumpet player. While living on the *Eleanor,* he spent many evenings in the cabin by himself practicing hymns and patriotic music. Sometimes, out on the grounds, if he had a few minutes to kill, he would go below and practice. One afternoon, blundering around the Hell Hole in a thick summer fog, he grew tired of cranking the foghorn and got out his trumpet and stood on deck and played "The Star-Spangled Banner" over and over, alarming the crews of other draggers fogbound in the area, who thought an excursion boat was bearing down on them. After he went back to sleeping at home, he continued to practice in the evenings, but he had to give it up before long because of its effect on his mother's health.

"At that time," he says, "I was working hard on three hymns—'Up from the Grave He Arose,' 'There Is a Fountain Filled with Blood' and 'What a Friend We Have in Jesus.' I had 'What a Friend' just about where I wanted it. One evening after supper, I went in the parlor as usual and Ma was sitting on the settee reading the *Ladies' Home Journal* and I took the easy chair and went to work on 'What a Friend.' I was running through it the second or third time when, all of a sudden, Ma bust out crying. I laid my trumpet down and I asked her what in the world was the matter. 'That trumpet's what's the matter,' Ma said. 'It makes me sad.' She said it made her so sad she was having nightmares and losing weight."

Ellery walks with a pronounced stoop, favoring his left shoulder, where the rheumatism has settled, and he takes his time. "If I start to hustle and bustle," he says, "everything I eat repeats and repeats." He abhors hurry; he thinks that humanity in general has got ahead of itself. He once threatened to fire a man in his crew because he worked too hard. . . .

Ellery is about as self-sufficient as a man can be. He has no wife, no politics and no religion. "I put off getting married until I got me a good big boat," he says. "When I got the boat and got it paid for, the Depression struck. There's mighty few women that'll eat fish three times a day, and that's about all I had to offer. I kept putting it off until times got better. When times got better, I got the rheumatism.

And a man in his middle forties with the chronic rheumatism, there's not much of the old Romeo left in him."

Ellery is a member of only one organization. "I'm a Mason," he says. "Aside from that, the only thing I belong to is the human race." His father was a Republican and his mother is a Democrat; he says he has never put any dependence in either party and has never once voted for anybody. His family belongs to the Baptist Church; he says he has somehow managed to get along without it. "I enjoy hymns," he says. "I enjoy the old ones, the gloomy ones. I used to go to church just to hear the good old hymns, but the sermons finally drove me away."

12. Writing About a Place

Next to knowing how to write about people, you should know how to write about a place. People and places are the twin pillars on which most nonfiction is built. Every human event happens somewhere, and the reader wants to know what that "somewhere" was like.

In a few cases you will need only a paragraph or two to sketch the setting of an event. But more often you will need to evoke the mood of a whole neighborhood or town to give texture to the story you are telling. And in certain cases, such as the travel piece itself—that perennial form in which you recount how you lived on a houseboat in Kashmir or crossed the Sahara by bus—descriptive detail will be the main substance.

Whatever the proportion, it would seem to be relatively easy. The dismal truth is that it is very hard. It must be hard because it is in this area that most writers—professional and amateur—produce not only their worst work, but work that is just plain terrible.

The terrible work has nothing to do with some terrible flaw of character. On the contrary, it results from the virtue of enthusiasm. Nobody turns so quickly into a bore as a traveler home from his travels. He enjoyed his trip so much that he wants to tell us all about it—and "all" is what we don't want to hear. We only want to hear some. What made his trip different from everybody else's? What can he tell us that we don't already know? We don't want him to describe every ride at Disneyland, or tell us that the Grand Canyon is awesome, or that Venice has canals. If one of the rides at Disneyland got stuck, or if somebody fell into the awesome Grand Canyon, *that* would be worth hearing about.

It is natural for all of us when we have gone to a certain place to feel that somehow we are the first people who ever went there or thought such sensitive thoughts about it. Fair enough —it is what keeps us going and validates our experience. Who can visit the Tower of London without musing on the wives of Henry VIII, or visit Egypt and not be moved by the size and antiquity of the pyramids?

But this is ground already covered by many people. As a writer you must keep a tight rein on your subjective self— the traveler touched by new sights and sounds and smells— and keep an objective eye on the reader. The article that records what you did every day on your trip will fascinate you because it was your trip. Will it fascinate the reader? Nine times out of ten it won't. The mere agglomeration of detail is no free pass to his interest. The detail must in some way be significant.

The other big trap is style. Nowhere else in nonfiction do writers use such syrupy words and groaning platitudes. Adjectives that you would squirm to use in conversation—"roseate," "wondrous," "fabled"—are common currency. Half the sights seen in a day's sightseeing are "quaint," especially windmills and covered bridges. They are certified for quaintness.

It is a style of soft words which under hard examination mean nothing, or which mean different things to different people: "attractive," "charming," "romantic." To write that "the city has its own attractiveness" is no help—every city does. And who will define "charm," except possibly the owner of a charm school? Or "romantic"? These are subjective concepts in the eye of the beholder. One man's romantic sunrise is another man's hangover.

Travelese is a land "where old meets new." I'm amazed at the number of places where old meets new. Old never meets old. The meeting occurs in the "twisting alleys" and "bustling thoroughfares" of storied Tangier or picturesque Zanzibar. This is terrain dotted with "byways," usually half-forgotten or at least hidden. It is a world where inanimate objects spring to transitive life: storefronts smile, buildings boast, ruins beckon and the very chimney tops sing their immemorial song of welcome. The clichés bloom with very fertility.

How can you overcome such fearful odds and write well about a place? My advice can be reduced to two principles— one of style, the other of substance.

First, choose your words with unusual care. If a phrase comes to you easily, look at it with deep suspicion—it's probably one of the innumerable clichés which have woven their way so tightly into the fabric of travel writing that it takes a special effort *not* to use them. Also resist straining for the luminous lyrical phrase to describe the wondrous waterfall. At best it will make you sound artificial—unlike yourself—and at worst pompous. Strive for fresh words and images. Leave "myriad" and their ilk to the poets. Leave "ilk" to anyone who will take it away.

As for substance, be intensely selective. If you are describing a beach, don't write that "the shore was scattered with rocks" or that "occasionally a seagull flew over." Shores have a tendency to be scattered with rocks and to be flown over by seagulls. Eliminate every such fact that is a known attribute: don't tell us that the sea had waves and that the sand was white. Find details that are significant. They may be important to your narrative. They may be unusual, or colorful, or comic, or entertaining. But make sure they are details that do useful work.

I'll give you some examples from various writers, widely different in temperament but alike in the effectiveness of the detail that they chose. The first is from an article by Joan Didion called "Some Dreamers of the Golden Dream." It is about a lurid crime that occurred in the San Bernardino Valley of California, and in this early passage the writer is taking us, as if in her own car, away from urban civilization to the lonely stretch of road where Lucille Miller's Volkswagen so unaccountably caught fire:

This is the California where it is easy to Dial-A-Devotion, but hard to buy a book. This is the country of the teased hair and the Capris and the girls for whom all life's promise comes down to a waltz-length white wedding dress and the birth of a Kimberly or a Sherry or a Debbi and a Tijuana divorce and a return to hairdressers' school. "We were just crazy kids," they say without regret, and look to the future. The future always looks good in the golden land, because no one remembers the past. Here is where the hot wind blows and the old ways do not seem relevant, where the divorce rate is double the national average and where one person in every 38 lives in a trailer. Here is the last stop for all those who come from somewhere else, for all those who drifted away from the cold and the past and the old ways. Here is where they are trying to find a new life style, trying to find it in the only places they know to look: the movies and the newspapers. The case of Lucille Marie Maxwell Miller is a tabloid monument to the new style.

Imagine Banyan Street first, because Banyan is where it happened. The way to Banyan is to drive west from San Bernardino out Foothill Boulevard, Route 66: past the Santa Fe switching yards, the Forty Winks Motel. Past the motel that is 19 stucco tepees: "SLEEP IN A WIGWAM—GET MORE FOR YOUR WAMPUM." Past Fontana Drag City and Fontana Church of the Nazarene and the Pit Stop A Go-Go; past Kaiser Steel, through Cucamonga, out to the Kapu Kai Restaurant-Bar and Coffee Shop, at the corner of Route 66

and Carnelian Avenue. Up Carnelian Avenue from the
Kapu Kai, which means "Forbidden Seas," the subdivision
flags whip in the harsh wind. "HALF-ACRE RANCHES! SNACK
BARS! TRAVERTINE ENTRIES! $95 DOWN." It is the trail of an
intention gone haywire, the flotsam of the New California.
But after a while the signs thin out on Carnelian Avenue,
and the houses are no longer the bright pastels of the
Springtime Home owners but the faded bungalows of the
people who grow a few grapes and keep a few chickens out
here, and then the hill gets steeper and the road climbs and
even the bungalows are few, and here—desolate, roughly
surfaced, lined with eucalyptus and lemon groves—is Banyan Street.

In only two paragraphs we have a feeling not only for the
tackiness of the New California landscape, with its stucco tepees
and instant housing and borrowed Hawaiian romance, but for
the pathetic impermanence of the lives and pretensions of the
people who have alighted there. All the details—statistics and
names and signs—are doing helpful work.

Concrete detail is also the anchor of John McPhee's prose.
McPhee has published more than a dozen books since 1964,
each different in subject, each such a gem of craftsmanship that
he is now regarded as one of America's finest nonfiction writers.
Coming into the Country, his book about Alaska, has a section
devoted to the quest for a possible new state capital. It takes
him only a few sentences to give us a sense of what's wrong with
the present capital, both as a place to live and as a place for
lawmakers to make good laws:

A pedestrian today in Juneau, head down and charging,
can be stopped for no gain by the wind. There are railings
along the streets by which senators and representatives can
haul themselves to work. Over the past couple of years, a
succession of wind gauges were placed on a ridge above the
town. They could measure velocities up to 200 miles per

hour. They did not survive. The taku winds tore them apart after driving their indicators to the end of the scale. The weather is not always so bad; but under its influence the town took shape, and so Juneau is a tight community of adjacent buildings and narrow European streets, adhering to its mountainsides and fronting the salt water. . . .

The urge to move the capital came over Harris during those two years [in the Alaska State Senate]. Sessions began in January and ran on at least three months, and Harris developed what he called "a complete sense of isolation— stuck there. People couldn't get at you. You were in a cage. You talked to the hard lobbyists every day. Every day the same people. What was going on needed more airing."

The oddity of the city, so remote from the ordinary American experience, is instantly clear. One possibility for the legislators was to move the capital to Anchorage. There at least nobody would feel that he was in an alien town. McPhee distills its essence in a paragraph that is brilliant both in detail and in metaphor:

Almost all Americans would recognize Anchorage, because Anchorage is that part of any city where the city has burst its seams and extruded Colonel Sanders. Anchorage is sometimes excused in the name of pioneering. Build now, civilize later. But Anchorage is not a frontier town. It is virtually unrelated to its environment. It has come in on the wind, an American spore. A large cookie cutter brought down on El Paso could lift something like Anchorage into the air. Anchorage is the northern rim of Trenton, the center of Oxnard, the ocean-blind precincts of Daytona Beach. It is condensed, instant Albuquerque.

Another kind of travel writing, the personal memoir, a rich form because it taps so many wells of childhood and growing up, also depends on the writer's ability to call back what made his neighborhood distinctive, his early life unique. One of my favorite examples is Alfred Kazin's *A Walker in the City*. The locale is Brownsville, a Jewish ghetto in Brooklyn, and the detail tends to be sensual. Smells, for instance, are evocative for Kazin. For another writer, what stirs a specific memory might be a sound, or the theme song of an old radio show.

Here is a fragment of Kazin's youth:

> It was the darkness and emptiness of the streets I liked most about Friday evening, as if in preparation for that day of rest and worship which the Jews greet "as a bride"—that day when the very touch of money is prohibited, all work, all travel, all household duties, even to the turning on and off of a light—Jewry had found its way past its tormented heart to some ancient still center of itself. I waited for the streets to go dark on Friday evening as other children waited for the Christmas lights. . . . When I returned home after three, the warm odor of a coffee cake baking in the oven, and the sight of my mother on her hands and knees scrubbing the linoleum on the dining room floor, filled me with such tenderness that I could feel my senses reaching out to embrace every single object in our household.
>
> My great moment came at six, when my father returned from work, his overalls smelling faintly of turpentine and shellac, white drops of silver paint still gleaming on his chin. Hanging his overcoat in the long dark hall that led into our kitchen, he would leave in one pocket a loosely folded copy of the New York *World;* and then everything that beckoned to me from that other hemisphere of my brain beyond the East River would start up from the smell of fresh newsprint and the sight of the globe on the front page. It was a paper that carried special associations for me with Brooklyn Bridge. They published the *World* under the green dome of Park Row overlooking the bridge; the fresh salt air of New York harbor lingered for me in the

smell of paint and damp newsprint in the hall. I felt that my father brought the outside straight into our house with each day's copy.

Another area where your success will rest on freshness of detail is the vast field of exploration and adventure, especially when it also involves the history of an obscure region and the reconstruction of events that happened long ago. For me the best hand at this difficult work is Alan Moorehead. I have followed him across much of Africa and Australia and Asia and the Pacific, always struck with admiration bordering on disbelief that he could collate such a wealth of present and past experience and write about it with seemingly effortless warmth.

His books *The White Nile* and *The Blue Nile* are marvels of craftsmanship. Though they deal with a huge gallery of men and women who sought the source of those rivers in the nineteenth century, bedeviled by hostile nature and hostile tribes, by illness and ignorance, by jurisdictional squabbles in the interior and back in England, all the characters are wonderfully alive, and so is Moorehead as a writer, stitching his own observations of Africa together with what he has extracted from the journals of the explorers who preceded him up the Nile long ago.

Moorehead's style is so uniformly pleasant that I could quote from almost any page of his books or articles. The following excerpt is as good as any because it is descriptive material of the kind that is ordinarily so susceptible to banalities and purple prose:

> Many years have gone by since I first flew up the valley of the upper Nile, starting the journey at Khartoum, in the Sudan, and ending it nearly two thousand miles away, at the source of the river, in Uganda. I was a war correspondent at the time, on my way from one campaign, in the western desert of Egypt, to another, in Ethiopia. Even then, when planes did not fly nearly so high as they do

today, there was not very much to be seen from the air
except the endless desert and the meandering green line
of the river, but there were frequent stops along the way,
and these I remember just as distinctly as one remembers
the islands on a long ocean voyage.

Before we started, we were held up for three or four days
at Khartoum with engine trouble. It was April, the hottest
time of the year—so hot, in fact, that it was slightly painful
just to touch the porcelain sides of your bathtub when you
got up in the morning. A fearsome sandstorm known as a
haboob was blowing, and it was only at the very end of the
long, torpid day that the town woke up at last. Each evening, about an hour before the light began to fail, I used to
walk down to the zoo with a book. The Khartoum Zoo is
quite unlike any other zoo in the world. It lies on the left
bank of the Blue Nile, just upstream from the point where
the White Nile comes in from the southern Sudan, and it
covers hardly more than two or three acres.

The animals and the birds do not have that vacant and
dispirited air that seems to overtake tropical creatures
when they are transported to cold climates in the north.
They have all been born here in this hothouse atmosphere,
and many of them are not kept in cages; they simply roam
about in their natural state, grazing on the grass and the
bushes or wading in the pond. At the hour when I used to
go to the zoo, there were hardly any visitors, and as I sat
there reading, the zebras, the antelopes and many kinds of
long-legged birds would gather around in a quiet and hesi-
tating way that was something between curiosity and fear.
It was very pleasant and very peaceful, and this made it all
the more surprising one evening when I looked up from
my book and found General de Gaulle standing before me.
He was wearing a pale-blue kepi and a tropical uniform,
and as I rose from my bench he saluted in a friendly, informal way and went off to see the giraffes. Heaven knows

what he was doing in that outlandish place. I saw him only twice more during the war—once at Casablanca, with Roosevelt and Churchill, and then during the Liberation of Paris, when he marched down the Champs-Elysées at the head of his men and we were all in tears.

Finally, let me come to that troublesome organism the travel piece itself. This is the article whose primary purpose is to describe a certain place—never mind such collateral purposes as telling a story or reconstructing a set of events. Practice writing this kind of article, and just because I call it a travel piece I don't mean that you have to go to Khartoum. Go to your local shopping mall, or bowling alley, or park. Or write about your vacation. But whatever place you write about, go there long enough or often enough to isolate the qualities that make it special. Usually this will be some combination of the place and the people who inhabit it. If it's your local bowling alley it will be a mixture of the atmosphere inside and the regular patrons. If it's a foreign city it will be some mixture of the ancient culture and its present populace. Try to find it.

A master of this feat of detection is the English author V. S. Pritchett, one of the best and most versatile of nonfiction writers. Consider what he squeezes out of a visit to Istanbul:

Istanbul has meant so much to the imagination that the reality shocks most travelers. We cannot get the sultans out of our minds. We half expect to find them still cross-legged and jewelled on their divans. We remember tales of the harem. The truth is that Istanbul has no glory except its situation. It is a city of steep, cobbled, noisy hills. . . .

Mostly the shops sell cloth, clothes, stockings, shoes, the Greek traders rushing out, with cloth unrolled, at any potential customer, the Turks passively waiting. Porters shout; everyone shouts; you are butted by horses, knocked sideways by loads of bedding, and, through all this, you see one of the miraculous sights of Turkey—a demure youth

carrying a brass tray suspended on three chains, and in the
exact center of the tray a small glass of red tea. He never
spills it; he maneuvers it through chaos to his boss, who is
sitting on the doorstep of his shop.

One realizes there are two breeds in Turkey: those who
carry and those who sit. No one sits quite so relaxedly,
expertly, beatifically as a Turk; he sits with every inch of his
body; his very face sits. He sits as if he inherited the art from
generations of sultans in the palace above Seraglio Point.
Nothing he likes better than to invite you to sit with him
in his shop or in his office with half a dozen other sitters: a
few polite inquiries about your age, your marriage, the sex
of your children, the number of your relations, and where
and how you live, and then, like the other sitters, you clear
your throat with a hawk that surpasses anything heard in
Lisbon, New York or Sheffield, and join the general silence.

I like the phrase "his very face sits"—just four short words,
but they convey an idea so fanciful that they take us by surprise.
They also tell us a great deal about Turks. I'll never be able to
visit Turkey again without noticing its sitters. With one quick
insight Pritchett has caught a whole national trait. This is the
essence of good writing about a place. Distill the important
from the immaterial.

I'm reminded by Pritchett's own nationality that the English
have long excelled at a distinctive form of travel writing that I
should mention before traveling on—the article that is less no-
table for what the writer extracts from a place than for what the
place extracts from him. New sights touch off thoughts that
would otherwise never have entered his mind. If travel is
broadening, it should broaden more than just our knowledge of,
say, how a Gothic cathedral looks or how the French make
wine. It should generate a whole constellation of new ideas
about how men and women work and play, raise their children,
worship their gods, live and die. Certainly the books written by
Britain's "desert eccentrics"—scholar-adventurers like Charles

Doughty and T. E. Lawrence, who chose to live among the Arabs—derive much of their strange power from the reflections born of surviving in so harsh and minimal an environment.

So when you write about a place, try to draw the best out of it. But if the process should work in reverse, let it draw the best out of you. In this sense, probably the finest travel book written by an American is *Walden,* though Thoreau only went a few miles out of town, and today a growing number of nonfiction writers are finding their voice by hitting the road, going back to the land or pondering the mysteries of nature.

No writer has been more creatively provoked by the search for modern America than Norman Mailer. Shrewd and witty insights about our latest values fly like sparks out of his books—typically, his book about the launching of Apollo 11, *Of a Fire on the Moon,* and about the faceless new breed of men who reared it and raised it into space. What did it all mean? Was the achievement stirring or sterile? Even Mailer isn't sure at the end, and Mailer is seldom at a loss for certitudes. But there has been much to think about along the way.

Let me leave you with him, then, on the eve of the launch, staring with "some portion of a million" rubberneckers across the water to the spaceship that would lift itself off its pad in the morning and take three men to the moon:

> In the distance she glowed for all the world like some white stone Madonna in the mountains, welcoming foot-sore travelers at dusk. Perhaps it was an unforeseen game of the lighting, but America had not had its movie premieres for nothing, nor its Rockettes in Radio City and 50 million squares tooling the tourist miles over the years to Big Town to buy a ticket to spectacle and back home again. If you were going to have a Hollywood premiere and arc lights, a million out to watch and a spaceship which looked across the evening flutter like the light on the Shrine of Our Lady outside any church in Brooklyn or Bay Ridge, then by God you might just as well have this spectacle on the pre-

miere trip to the moon. That deserved a searchlight or two!
There were new industries in America these years. After
five decades of suspense movies, and movies of the Wild
West, after the adventures of several generations of men in
two world wars and Korea and Vietnam, after 16 years of
Playboy and American iconization of the gravity-defying
breast and the sun-ripened buttock, after ten years of the
greatest professional football, after a hundred years and
more of a tradition that the frontier was open and would
never close, and after 20 more perplexing technological
years when prosperity came to nearly every White pocket,
and technology put out its plastic, its superhighways, its
supermarkets, its appliances, its suburbs, its smog, and its
intimation that the frontier was damn shut, shut like a
boulder on a rabbit burrow, America had erupted from this
pressure between its love of adventure and its fear that
adventure was completely shut down; America had
spewed out on the road. The country had become a nation
of campers, of cars toting trailers, of cars pulling tent-trail-
ers, of truck-campers, top-of-car tent packs, Volkswagen
buses converted to ambulatory bedrooms, jeeps with Chic
Sale houses built on the back, Land-Rovers with bunks,
Broncos with more bunks—any way a man could get out of
the house with his buddies or his family or his grandmother, and take to the road and find some ten by twenty
feet of grass not posted, not tenanted, and not too muddy,
he would camp. All over America in the summer the night
fields were now filled with Americans sleeping on air mat-
tresses which reposed on plastic cloth floors of plastic cloth
tents—what a sweet smell of Corporate Chemical, what a
vat and void to mix with all the balmy fermy chlorophylls
and pollens of nature! America the Sanitary, and America
the Wild, went out to sleep in the woods, Sanitary-Lobe and
Wild-Lobe nesting neatly together, schizophrenic twins in
the skull case of the good family American.

13. Bits & Pieces

This is a chapter of scraps and morsels—small admonitions on many points which I have collected under one, as they say, umbrella.

VERBS. Use active verbs unless there is no comfortable way to get around using a passive verb. The difference between an active-verb style and a passive-verb style—in pace, clarity and vigor—is the difference between life and death for a writer.

"Joe hit him" is strong. "He was hit by Joe" is weak. The first is short and vivid and direct; it leaves no doubt about who did what. The second is necessarily longer and it has an insipid quality; something was done by somebody to someone else. A style which consists mainly of passive constructions, especially if the sentences are long, saps the reader's energy. He is never quite certain of what is being perpetrated by whom and on whom.

I use "perpetrated" because it's the kind of word that passive-tense writers are fond of. They prefer long words of Latin origin to short Anglo-Saxon words—which compounds their trouble and makes their sentences still more glutinous. Short is generally better than long. (Of the 701 words in Lincoln's Second Inaugural Address, a marvel of economy in itself, 505 are words of one syllable and 122 are words of two syllables.)

Verbs are the most important of all your tools. They push the sentence forward and give it momentum. Active verbs push hard; passive verbs tug fitfully. Most verbs also carry somewhere in their imagery or in their sound a suggestion of what they mean: flail, poke, dazzle, squash, beguile, pamper, swagger, wheedle, vex. I would bet that no other language has such a vast supply of verbs so bright with color. Don't choose one that is dull or merely serviceable. Make active verbs activate your sentences, and try to avoid the kind that need an appended preposition or two to complete their work. Don't "set up" a business that you can establish. Don't "come upon" an object that you can discover, or "take hold of " one that you can grab. Don't "put up with" pain; bear it.

Cultivate this rich crop. And if you want to see how active verbs give vitality and flair to the written word, don't just go back to Hemingway or Thurber or Thoreau. I commend the King James Bible and William Shakespeare.

ADVERBS. Most adverbs are unnecessary. You will clutter your sentence and annoy the reader if you choose a verb that has a precise meaning and then add an adverb that carries the same meaning. Don't tell us that the radio blared loudly— "blare" connotes loudness. Don't write that someone clenched his teeth tightly—there is no other way to clench teeth. Again and again in careless writing, self-sufficient verbs are weakened by redundant adverbs.

So are countless adjectives and other parts of speech: "Totally flabbergasted," "effortlessly easy," "slightly spartan." The beauty of "flabbergasted" is that it implies an astonishment that is total; I can't picture anyone being partly flabbergasted. If an action is so easy as to be effortless, use "effortless." And what is "slightly spartan"? Perhaps a monk's cell with wall-to-wall carpeting.

Don't use adverbs unless they do some work. If an athlete

loses a game because he played badly, "badly" gives us the helpful information that he didn't play well. But spare us the news that he moped dejectedly and that the winner grinned widely.

ADJECTIVES. Most adjectives are also unnecessary. Like adverbs, they are sprinkled into sentences by writers who don't stop to think that the concept is already in the noun. This kind of prose is littered with precipitous cliffs and lacy spiderwebs and doleful mourners and friendly smiles. It is also littered with adjectives denoting the color of an object whose color is well known: yellow daffodils and brownish dirt. If you want to make a value judgment about daffodils, choose an adjective like "garish." If you're in a section of the country where the dirt is red, feel free to mention the red dirt. These adjectives would do a job that the noun wouldn't be doing.

Redundant adjectives are only part of the problem. Most writers sow adjectives almost unconsciously into the soil of their prose to make it more lush and pretty. The sentences become longer and longer as they fill up with stately elms and graceful boughs and frisky kittens and sleepy lagoons. This is adjective-by-habit, and it's a habit you should stop. Not every oak has to be gnarled, every detective hard-bitten. The adjective that exists solely as decoration is a self-indulgence for the writer and an obstacle for the reader.

Again, the rule is simple: make your adjectives do work that needs to be done. "He looked at the gray sky and the black clouds and decided to sail back to the harbor." The darkness of the sky is the reason for the decision. If it's important to tell the reader that a house was drab or that a girl was beautiful, by all means use "drab" and "beautiful." They will have their proper power because you have learned to use adjectives sparsely.

LITTLE QUALIFIERS. Prune out the small words that qualify how you feel and how you think and what you saw: "a bit," "a little," "sort of," "kind of," "rather," "quite," "very," "too," "pretty much" "in a very real sense," and dozens more. They dilute both your style and your persuasiveness.

Don't say you were a bit confused and sort of tired and a little depressed and somewhat annoyed. Be tired. Be confused. Be depressed. Be annoyed. Don't hedge your prose with little timidities. Good writing is lean and confident.

Don't say you weren't too happy because the hotel looked pretty expensive. Say you weren't happy because the hotel looked expensive. Don't tell us that you were quite fortunate. How fortunate is that?

Don't describe an event as rather spectacular or very awesome. Words like "spectacular" and "awesome" don't submit to measurement. "Very" is a useful word to achieve emphasis, but far more often it is clutter. There is no need to call someone very methodical. Either he is methodical or he isn't.

The larger point here is one of authority. Every little qualifier whittles away some fraction of trust on the part of the reader. He wants a writer who believes in himself and in what he is saying. Don't diminish this belief. Don't be kind of bold. Be bold.

PUNCTUATION. These are brief thoughts on punctuation, in no way intended as a primer. If you don't know how to punctuate—and many college students still don't—get a grammar book.

The Period. There's not much to be said about the period except that most writers don't reach it soon enough. If you find yourself hopelessly mired in a long sentence, it's probably because you are trying to make the sentence do more than it can reasonably do—perhaps express two dissimilar thoughts. The quickest way out is to break the long sentence into two short sentences, or even three. There is no minimum length for a sentence that is acceptable in the eyes of man and God. Among good writers it is the short sentence that predominates, and don't tell me about Norman Mailer—he's a genius. If you want to write long sentences, be a genius. Or at least make sure that the sentence is under control from beginning to end, in syntax and punctuation, so that the reader knows where he is at every step of the winding trail.

The Exclamation Point. Don't use it unless you must to achieve a certain effect. It has a gushy aura—the breathless excitement of a debutante commenting on an event that was exciting only to her: "Daddy says I must have had too much champagne!" "But honestly, I just could have danced all night!" We have all suffered more than our share of these sentences in which an exclamation point knocks us over the head with how cute or wonderful something was. Instead, construct your sentence so that the order of the words will put the emphasis where you want it. Also resist using the exclamation point to notify the reader that you are making a joke or being ironic. "It never occurred to me that the water pistol might be loaded!" The reader is annoyed by your reminder that this was a comical moment. He is also robbed of the pleasure of making the discovery himself. Humor is best achieved by understatement, and there's nothing subtle about an exclamation point.

The Semicolon. There is a nineteenth-century mustiness that hangs over the semicolon. We associate it with the carefully balanced sentences, the judicious weighing of "on the one hand" and "on the other hand," of Conrad and Thackeray and Hardy. Therefore it should be used sparingly by writers of nonfiction today. Yet I notice that it turns up often in the excerpts that I have quoted in this book, and I have used it here myself more than I ordinarily do, mainly for the classic purpose of balancing pro and con, or of weighing two sides of the same problem. Still, the semicolon does bring the reader, if not to a halt, at least to a considerable pause. So use it with discretion, remembering that it will slow to a Victorian pace the twentieth-century momentum that you are striving for, and rely instead on the period and the dash.

The Dash. Somehow this invaluable tool is widely regarded as not quite proper—a bumpkin at the genteel dinner table of good English. But it has full membership and will get you out of many tight corners. The dash is used in two different ways. One is to amplify or justify in the second part of the sentence a thought that you have stated in the first part. "We decided to keep going—it was only 100 miles more and we could get there in time for dinner." By its very shape the dash pushes the sentence ahead and explains why they decided to keep going. The other use involves two dashes, which set apart a parenthetical thought within a longer sentence. "She told me to get in the car—she had been after me all summer to have a haircut—and we drove silently into town." An explanatory detail that might otherwise have had to go into a separate sentence is dispatched along the way.

The Colon. The colon has begun to look even more antique than the semicolon, and many of its functions have been taken over by the dash. But it still serves well its pure role of bringing your sentence to a brief halt before you plunge into, say, a quotation or an itemized list. "The brochure said that the ship would stop at the following ports: Oran, Algiers, Naples, Brindisi, Piraeus, Istanbul and Beirut." You can't beat the colon for work like that.

MOOD CHANGERS. Learn to alert the reader as early as possible in a sentence to any change in mood from the previous sentence. At least a dozen words will do this job for you: "but," "yet," "however," "nevertheless," "still," "instead," "thus," "therefore," "meanwhile," "now," "later," "today," "subsequently" and several more. I can't overstate how much easier it is for the reader if you start with "but" when you're shifting direction, or, conversely, how much harder it is if he must wait until the end to realize that you are now in a different gear.

Many of us were taught that no sentence should begin with "but." If that's what you learned, unlearn it—there is no stronger word at the start. It announces total contrast with what has gone before, and the reader is primed for the change. If you need relief from too many sentences beginning with "but," switch to "however." It is, however, a weaker word and there-fore needs careful placement. Don't start a sentence with "how-ever"—it hangs there like a wet dishrag. And don't end with "however"—by that time it has lost its "howeverness." Put it as early as you reasonably can—as I did three sentences ago. Its abruptness then becomes a virtue.

"Yet" does almost the same job as "but," though its meaning is closer to "nevertheless." Either of these words at the begin-ning of a sentence—"Yet he decided to go" or "Nevertheless he decided to go"—can replace a whole long phrase which summa-rizes what the reader has just been told: "Despite the fact that all these dangers had been pointed out to him, he decided to go." Look for all the places where one of these short words will quickly convey the same mood and meaning as a long and dismal clause. "Instead I took the train." "Still I had to admire him." "Thus I learned how to smoke." "It was therefore easy to meet him." "Meanwhile I had talked to John." What a vast amount of huffing and puffing these pivotal words save! (The exclamation point is to show that I really mean it.)

As for "meanwhile," "now," "today" and "later," what they also save is confusion, for writers often change their time con-text without remembering to tip the reader off. "Now I know better." "Today you can't find such an item." "Later I found out why." Always make sure that the reader is oriented. And do it as soon as possible whenever you change your orientation.

CONTRACTIONS. Your style will obviously be warmer and truer to your personality if you use contractions like "I'll" and "won't" when they fit comfortably into what you are writing. "I'll be glad to see them if they don't get mad" is less stiff than "I will be glad to see them if they do not get mad." There is no rule against such informality—trust your ear and your instincts.

I only suggest avoiding one form—"I'd," "he'd," "we'd," etc.—because "I'd" can mean both "I had" and "I would," and the reader must often get well into a sentence before learning which meaning it is. Frequently it turns out to be not the one he thought it was.

OVERSTATEMENT. "The living room looked as if an atomic bomb had gone off there," writes the inexperienced writer, describing what he saw on Sunday morning after a Saturday night party that got out of hand. Well, we all know that he's exaggerating to make a droll point, but we also know that an atomic bomb *didn't* go off there, or any other bomb except maybe a water bomb. "I felt as if ten 747 jets were flying through my brain," he says, "and I seriously considered jumping out the window and killing myself." These verbal high jinks can get just so high—and I'm already well over the limit—before the reader feels an overpowering drowsiness. It is like being trapped with a man who can't stop reciting limericks. Don't overstate. You didn't really consider jumping out the window. Life has more than enough truly horrible funny situations. Let the humor sneak up so that we hardly hear it coming.

CREDIBILITY. Credibility is just as fragile for a writer as for a President. Don't inflate an incident to make it more flamboyant or bizarre than it actually was. If the reader catches you in just one bogus statement that you are trying to pass off as true, everything that you write thereafter will be suspect. It is too great a risk, and not worth taking.

CONCEPT NOUNS. Nouns that express a concept are commonly used in bad writing instead of verbs that tell what somebody did. Here are three typical dead sentences:
"The common reaction is incredulous laughter."
"Bemused cynicism isn't the only response to the old system."

"The current campus hostility is a symptom of the change."
What is so eerie about these sentences is that they have no
people in them. They also have no working verbs—only "is" or
"isn't." The reader can't visualize anybody performing some
task. The meaning all lies in impersonal nouns that embody a
vague concept: "reaction," "cynicism," "response," "hostility."
Turn these cold sentences around. Get people doing things:

"Most people just laugh with disbelief."

"Some people respond to the old system by turning cynical;
others say . . ."

"It's easy to notice the change—you can see how angry all the
students are."

My revised sentences aren't jumping with vigor, partly because the material that I'm trying to knead into shape is shape-
less dough. But at least they have real people and real verbs.
Don't get caught holding a bag that doesn't have anything in it
but abstract nouns. You'll sink to the bottom of the lake and
never be seen again.

CREEPING NOUNISM. This is a new disease that strings two
or three nouns together where one will do. Nobody goes broke
in America now; we have money problem areas. It no longer
rains; we have precipitation activity. Choose one noun, preferably one that is short and specific. Choose it carefully and it will
do the job.

SEXISM. Probably the most vexing new question for writers
is what to do about the "he-she" pronoun. The feminist movement has demonstrated how much sexism lurks in our language,
not only in the bothersome "he," but in the hundreds of words
that carry an invidious meaning or some overtone of judgment.
They are words which patronize ("gal"), or which imply second-
class status ("poetess"), or which are deliberately prurient
("divorcée," "coed," "blonde") and which are seldom applied to
men. Men get mugged; a woman who gets mugged is a shapely

stewardess or a pert brunette. Good writers and editors are now pushing these stereotypes out of the language.

A thornier problem is raised by the feminists' annoyance with words that contain "man," such as "chairman" and "spokesman." Their point, of course, is that women can chair a committee as well as a man and that they are equally good at spoking. Hence the flurry of new words like "chairperson" and "spokeswoman." These makeshift words served a larger purpose throughout the 1970s of raising our consciousness about sex discrimination both in words and in attitudes. But in the end they are makeshift words, perhaps hurting the cause more than helping it. My own feeling is that they will now begin to fade away. "Chairman" is an honorable title, and I prefer it to "chairperson" or "chairwoman." So, I think, will most of the women in the 1980s who become chairman of a company or a board. The main battle—to prove that women can assume traditionally male jobs—is rapidly being won.

This still leaves the problem of the pronoun. Obviously "he" and "him" and "his" are words that rankle. "Every employee should decide what he thinks is best for him and his dependents." What are we to do about these countless sentences? One solution is to turn them into the plural: "All employees should decide what they think is best for them and their dependents." But this cure is good only in small doses. Plurals are weaker than singulars. The singular is particular and concrete, and a style that converts every "he" into a "they" will quickly turn to mush.

Another common solution is to use "or": "Every employee should decide what he or she thinks is best for him or her." But, again, it can only be used sparingly. Often a writer will find several situations in an article where he or she can use "he or she," or "him or her," if it seems natural. By "natural" I mean that the writer is serving notice that he (or she) has the problem in mind and is trying his (or her) best within reasonable limits. But let's face it: the English language is stuck with the generic "he" ("Man shall not live by bread alone"). To turn every "he" into a "he or she," and every "his" into a "his or her," would thicken the language and make it much harder to read. This book, for instance, would be longer and drearier if I used "he or she" with every mention of "the writer" and "the reader." I reject "he/she" altogether; the slant has no place in good English.

The best solutions simply eliminate male pronouns and connotations by altering some component of the sentence. "We" is a useful substitute for "he"; "the" can often replace "his"; general nouns can replace specific nouns: (A) "First he notices what's happening to his kids and he blames it on his neighborhood." (B) "First we notice what's happening to our kids and we blame it on the neighborhood." (A) "Doctors often neglect their wives and children." (B) "Doctors often neglect their families." Countless sins can be erased by such small changes.

The pedants, of course, have other solutions. (Like the poor, the pedants are always with us.) They have proposed various unisex pronouns, deriving from Nordic or Anglo-Saxon roots that only they have dug up, which they claim would fall easily into our speech if we just started teaching them in our schools and writing them in our writings. One of their typical candidates is "thon," a third-person pronoun that applies to either gender and has a handy possessive ("thons") and reflexive ("thonself"). Maybe I don't speak for the average American, but I very much doubt that thon wants that word in thons language or that thon would use it thonself. This is not how language changes.

PARAGRAPHS. Keep your paragraphs short, especially if you are writing for a newspaper or a magazine that sets its type in a narrow width. This is purely visual and psychological advice.

Short paragraphs put air around what you write and make it look inviting, whereas one long chunk of type can discourage the reader from even starting to read. A newspaper paragraph generally shouldn't have more than two or three sentences. You may worry that such frequent paragraphing will damage the logical development of your idea. (Obviously *The New Yorker* is obsessed by this fear—a reader can go for several columns without relief.) Don't worry. The gains far outweigh the dangers.

WRITING IS NOT A CONTEST. Every writer is starting from a different point and is bound for a different destination. Yet many writers are paralyzed by the thought that they are competing with everybody else who is trying to write and is presumably doing it better. This can often happen, for instance, in a writing class. Inexperienced students are chilled to find themselves in the same class with students whose byline has appeared in the college newspaper. But writing for the college paper is no great credential; in fact, I have often found that the hares who write for the paper are overtaken by the tortoises who move resolutely toward the goal of mastering the craft. The same fear cripples the lonely free-lance writer, who sees the work of other writers appearing in magazines while his own keeps returning in the mail. Forget the competition and go at your own pace. Ultimately your only contest is with yourself.

THE SUBCONSCIOUS MIND. Your subconscious mind does more writing than you think. Often you will spend a whole day trying to fight your way out of some verbal thicket in which you seem to be tangled beyond salvation. Surprisingly often a solution will occur to you the next morning when you plunge back in. While you slept, your writer's mind didn't. To some extent a writer is always working. Stay alert to the currents around you. Much of what you see and hear will come back, having percolated for days or even months through your subconscious mind, just when your conscious mind, laboring over the typewriter, needs it.

DICTATION. Much of the "writing" done in America is done by dictation. Administrators, executives, managers, bureaucrats and other officials think in terms of using their time efficiently. To them the quickest way of getting something "written" is to dictate it to a secretary and never look at it. This is false economy—they save a few hours and blow their whole personality. Dictated sentences tend to be pompous, sloppy and redundant. If an executive is so busy that he can't avoid dictating, he should at least find time to edit what he has dictated, crossing words out and putting words in, making sure that what he finally writes is a true reflection of who he is, especially if it's a document that will go to a large number of readers who will judge him as a person on the basis of his style.

THE HUMAN CONDITION. Let's get rid of "the human condition."

14. Science Writing and Technical Writing

Take a class of writing students in a liberal arts college, tell them that their next assignment is to write on some aspect of science, and a pitiful moan will go around the room. "No! Not science!" the moan says. "Don't make us enter that dread region whose mysteries can only be fathomed by other scientists."

My sympathy is with them. I'm not much farther along myself than James Thurber's grandmother, who thought that "electricity was dripping invisibly all over the house" from wall sockets. But as a writer I know that a complex subject can be made as accessible to the layman as a simple subject. It's just a question of putting one sentence after another. The "after," however, is unusually important. Nowhere else must you work so hard to write sentences that form a linear sequence. This is no place for fanciful leaps or implied truths. Fact and deduction are the ruling family.

The assignment that I gave to students was a seemingly primitive one. I just asked them to describe how something works. I didn't care about a seductive lead or a surprise ending or any connecting devices. I only wanted them to tell me, say, how a sewing machine does what it does, or a bicycle, or why an apple falls down, or how the eye tells the brain what it sees. Any process will do, and science can be defined loosely to include technology, medicine and nature.

It is a tenet of journalism that "the reader knows nothing." As tenets go, it's not too complimentary, but the writer will forget it at his peril. You just can't assume that people know what you think any boob knows, or that they still remember what has once been explained to them. I doubt, for instance, if I could get into one of those life jackets that hundreds of airline stewardesses have demonstrated to me: something about pulling two toggle knobs sharply downward (or is it sideways?). I can translate the stewardesses' language—when they say "Do not effectuate these steps until you have vacated the aircraft as this will markedly increase your personal difficulty in disembarking," they mean "Don't blow the thing up or you won't get out." But what about those *other* steps—the straps that I "simply" have to slip into, the snaps I "simply" have to snap? I couldn't effectuate them if my life depended on it—as, some day, it probably will.

Describing how a process works is valuable for two reasons. First it forces you to make sure that *you* know how it works. Then it forces you to make sure that the reader will understand it as clearly as you do. In fact, I found it to be a breakthrough assignment for many students who just couldn't disentangle themselves from vagueness, clutter and disorderly thinking.

One of them, a sophomore still immobilized in these swamps at mid-term—a bright mind spraying the page with fuzzy thoughts—was in a joyful mood when he brought me his piece on how a fire extinguisher works. I was dubious. But the piece was absolutely lucid. It explained how different kinds of fires are specifically attacked by different kinds of extinguishers. It moved with utmost simplicity and logic. I was elated by his overnight change into a writer who had learned the secret of writing sequentially. By the end of his junior year he had written and published a "how to" book that sold better than any book *I* had written, and he has since published several more.

Many other students who were equally adrift went through the same miracle cure and have written with clarity ever since. For the principle of science writing applies to *all* nonfiction writing. It's the principle of leading a reader who knows nothing, step by step, to a grasp of the subject. Once you learn it, remember it in every article that you write.

Let me tilt the linear example by 90 degrees and ask you to imagine science writing as an upside-down pyramid. Start at the bottom with the one fact that a reader must know before he can learn any more. The second sentence broadens what was stated first, making the pyramid wider, and the third sentence broadens the second, so that gradually you can move beyond mere fact into significance and speculation —how a new discovery alters what was previously known, what new avenues of research it might open, where the research might be applied. There is no limit to how wide the inverted pyramid can become, but the reader will understand the broad implications only if he starts with a narrow fact.

A good example is a recent article that ran on page 1 of the *New York Times,* by Harold M. Schmeck, Jr.

WASHINGTON—There was a chimpanzee in California with a talent for playing ticktacktoe. Its trainers were delighted with this evidence of learning, but they were even more impressed by something else. They found they could tell from the animal's brain whether any particular move would be right or wrong. It depended on the chimpanzee's state of attention. When the trained animal was properly attentive, he made the right move.

Well, that's a reasonably interesting fact. But why is it worth page 1 of the *Times?* Paragraph 2 tells me:

The significant fact was that scientists were able to recognize that state. By elaborate computer analysis of brain wave signals they were learning to distinguish what might be called "states of mind."

But hadn't this been possible before?

This was far more ambitious than simply detecting gross states of arousal, drowsiness or sleep. It was a new step toward understanding how the brain works.

How is it a new step?

The chimpanzee and the research team at the University of California at Los Angeles have graduated from the ticktacktoe stage, but the work with brain waves is continuing. It has already revealed some surprising insights to the brain's behavior during space flight. It shows promise of application to social and domestic problems on earth and even to improvements in human learning.

Good. I could hardly ask a broader application of the research: space, human problems and the cognitive process. But is it an isolated effort? No indeed.

It is part of the large ferment of modern brain research in progress in laboratories throughout the United States and abroad. Involved are all manner of creatures from men and monkeys to rats and mice, goldfish, flatworms and Japanese quail.

I begin to see the total context. But what is the purpose?

The ultimate goal is to understand the human brain— that incredible three-pound package of tissue that can imagine the farthest reaches of the universe and the ultimate core of the atom but cannot fathom its own functioning. Each research project bites off a little piece of an immense puzzle.

So now I know where the chimp at U.C.L.A. fits into the spec-
trum of international science. Knowing this, I'm ready to go
back and learn about his particular contribution.

In the case of the chimpanzee being taught to play ticktacktoe, even the trained eye could see nothing beyond the
ordinary in the wavy lines being traced on paper to represent electrical waves from an animal's brain. But through
analysis by computer it was possible to tell which traces
showed that the animal was about to make the right move
and which preceded a mistake.

An important key was the system of computer analysis
developed largely by Dr. John Hanley. The state of mind
that always foreshadowed a correct answer was one that
might be described as trained attentiveness. Without the
computer's ability to analyze the huge complexities of the
recorded brain waves, the "signatures" of such states could
not have been detected.

The article goes on for four columns to describe potential uses
of the research—measuring causes of domestic tension, for instance, or reducing the rush-hour stress of drivers—and eventually it touches on work being done in many corners of the world
and in various pockets of medicine and psychology. But it
started with one chimpanzee playing ticktacktoe.

You can take much of the mystery out of science writing by
helping the reader to identify with the scientific work being
done. This means, once again, looking for the human element
—and if you have to settle for a chimpanzee, at least that's the
next-highest rung on the Darwinian ladder.

One obvious human element is yourself. Use your own experience to connect the reader to some mechanism that also
touches his life. In the following article on memory and how it
operates, which ran in *Life,* note how the writer, Will Bradbury, gives us at the start a personal handle with which to grab
an intricate subject:

Even now I see the dark cloud of sand before it hits my eyes, hear my father's calm voice urging me to cry the sting away, and feel anger and humiliation burn in my chest. More than 30 years have passed since that moment when a playmate, fighting for my toy ambulance, tossed a handful of sand in my face. Yet the look of the sand and ambulance, the sound of my father's voice and the throb of my bruised feelings all remain sharp and clear today. They are the very first things I can remember, the first bits of visual, verbal and emotional glass imbedded in the mosaic I have come to know as *me* by what is certainly the brain's most essential function—memory.

Without this miracle function that enables us to store and recall information, the brain's crucial systems for waking and sleeping, for expressing how we feel about things and for performing complicated acts could do little more than fumble with sensory inputs of the moment. Nor would man have a real feeling of self, for he would have no gallery of the past to examine, learn from, enjoy and, when necessary, hide away in. Yet after thousands of years of theorizing, of reading and misreading his own behavioral quirks, man is just beginning to have some understanding of the mysterious process that permits him to break and store bits of passing time.

One problem has been to decide what memory is and what things have it. Linseed oil, for example, has a kind of memory. Once exposed to light, even if only briefly, it will change consistency and speed the *second* time it is exposed. It will "remember" its first encounter with the light. Electronic and fluidic circuits also have memory of a more sophisticated kind. Built into computers, they are able to store and retrieve extraordinary amounts of information. And the human body has at least four kinds of memory. . . .

That's a fine lead. Who doesn't possess some cluster of vivid images that he can recall from an inconceivably early age? The reader is eager to learn how such a feat of storage and retrieval is accomplished. The example of the linseed oil is just piquant enough to make us wonder what "memory" really is, and then the writer reverts to the human frame of reference, for it is man who has built the computer circuits and who has four kinds of memory himself.

Another method is to weave a scientific story around some-one else. This is the continuing appeal of the articles called "Annals of Medicine" that Berton Roueché has long been writing in *The New Yorker.* They are detective stories, almost always involving a victim—some ordinary person struck by a mystifying ailment—and a gumshoe as obsessed as Sam Spade with finding the villain. Here's how one of them begins:

> At about 8 o'clock on Monday morning, Sept. 25, 1944, a ragged, aimless old man of 82 collapsed on the sidewalk on Dey Street, near the Hudson Terminal. Innumerable people must have noticed him, but he lay there alone for several minutes, dazed, doubled up with abdominal cramps, and in an agony of retching. Then a policeman came along. Until the policeman bent over the old man he may have supposed that he had just a sick drunk on his hands; wanderers dropped by drink are common in that part of town in the early morning. It was not an opinion that he could have held for long. The old man's nose, lips, ears and fingers were sky-blue.

By noon, eleven blue men have been admitted to nearby hospitals. But never fear—Dr. Ottavio Pellitteri, field epidemiologist, is quickly on the scene and telephoning Dr. Morris Greenberg at the Bureau of Preventable Diseases. Slowly the two men piece together fragments of evidence that seem to defy medical history until the case is at last nailed down and the villain identified as a type of poisoning so rare that many standard texts on toxicology don't even mention it.

Roueché's secret is as old as the art of storytelling. We are in on a chase and a mystery. But he doesn't start with the medical history of poisoning, or talk about standard texts on toxicology. He gives us a man—and not only a man but a blue one.

Another way of helping the reader to understand unfamiliar scientific facts is to relate them to sights that he *is* familiar with. Reduce the abstract principle to an image that he can visualize. Moshe Safdie, the architect who conceived Habitat, the innovative housing complex at Montreal's Expo 67, explains in his book, *Beyond Habitat,* that man would build better than he does if he took the time to see how nature does the job, since "nature makes form, and form is a by-product of evolution":

> One can study plant and animal life, rock and crystal formations, and discover the reasons for their particular form. The nautilus has evolved so that when its shell grows, its head will not get stuck in the opening. This is known as gnomonic growth; it results in the spiral formation. It is, mathematically, the only way it can grow.
>
> The same is true of achieving strength with a particular material. Look at the wings of a vulture, at its bone formation. A most intricate three-dimensional geometric pattern has evolved, a kind of space frame, with very thin bones that get thicker at the ends. The main survival problem for the vulture is to develop strength in the wing (which is under tremendous bending movement when the bird is flying) without building up weight, as that would limit its mobility. Through evolution the vulture has the most efficient structure one can imagine—a space frame in bone.

"For each aspect of life there are responses of form," Safdie writes, noting that the maple and the elm have wide leaves to absorb the maximum amount of sun for survival in a temperate climate, whereas the olive tree has a leaf that rotates because it must preserve moisture and can't absorb heat, and the cactus turns itself perpendicular to light. We may not know anything about botany, but we can all picture a maple leaf and a cactus plant. With every hard principle Safdie gives us a simple illustration:

> Economy and survival are the two key words in nature. Examined out of context, the neck of the giraffe seems uneconomically long, but it is economical in view of the fact that most of the giraffe's food is high on the tree. . . . Beauty as we understand it, and as we admire it in nature, is never arbitrary. The color and shape of flowers directly relate to their ability to attract insects; the color and formation of insects relate to their ability to camouflage themselves against the background of flowers.

Another way of making science accessible is to write like a person and not like a scientist. It's the same old question of warmth, of being yourself. Just because you are dealing with a scholarly discipline that is usually reported in a style of dry pedantry is no reason why you shouldn't write in good fresh English. Loren Eiseley is an example of a naturalist who refused to be cowed by nature as he passed on to us—in *The Immense Journey*—not only his knowledge but his enthusiasms:

> I have long been an admirer of the octopus. The cephalopods are very old, and they have slipped, protean, through many shapes. They are the wisest of the mollusks, and I have always felt it to be just as well for us that they never came ashore, but—there are other things that have.
>
> There is no need to be frightened. It is true that some of the creatures are odd, but I find the situation rather heartening than otherwise. It gives one a feeling of confidence to see nature still busy with experiments, still dynamic, and not through or satisfied because a Devonian fish managed to end as a two-legged character with a straw hat. There are other things brewing and growing in the oceanic vat. It

pays to know this. It pays to know there is just as much future as past. The only thing that doesn't pay is to be sure of man's own part in it.

Or take this passage from *The Lives of a Cell*, by Lewis Thomas, a biologist by training but a natural writer:

A solitary ant, afield, cannot be considered to have much of anything on his mind; indeed, with only a few neurons strung together by fibers, he can't be imagined to have a mind at all, much less a thought. He is more like a ganglion on legs. Four ants together, or ten, encircling a dead moth on a path, begin to look more like an idea. They fumble and shove, gradually moving the food toward the Hill, but as though by blind chance. It is only when you watch the dense mass of thousands of ants, crowded together around the Hill, blackening the ground, that you begin to see the whole beast, and now you observe it thinking, planning, calculating. It is an intelligence, a kind of live computer, with crawling bits for its wits.

At a stage in the construction, twigs of a certain size are needed, and all the members forage obsessively for twigs of just this size. Later, when outer walls are to be finished, thatched, the size must change, and as though given orders by telephone, all the workers shift the search to the new twigs. If you disturb the arrangement of a part of the Hill, hundreds of ants will set it vibrating, shifting, until it is put right again. Distant sources of food are somehow sensed, and long lines, like tentacles, reach out over the ground, up over walls, behind boulders, to fetch it in.

I have quoted from so many writers, writing about so many different facets of our physical world, to show that they all come across primarily as people, finding a common thread of humanity between themselves and their specialty and their readers.

They all write cleanly and without pretense; they all use vivid
images from the vocabulary of everyday life. They aren't scared
by their subject. On the contrary, they seem to be relaxed and
having a good time. You also can achieve this rapport.

Though I have used science as a demonstration model, the
same principles apply to any field where the reader must be led
across territory that is new and forbidding: business and
finance, medicine and public health, government and consumerism, energy and nuclear power, ecology and architecture.
Dozens of complex professions and new technologies await the
writer who can learn to describe them clearly. Only through
clear writing can the rest of us ponder our future and make
educated choices in areas where we have little or no education.

15. Writing in Your Job

Although this is a book about writing, it is not meant just for "writers." Its points are valid for all the people who have to do some writing just to get along in their job. The interoffice memo and the marketing analysis, for instance, are forms of writing, and many a career rises or falls on the ability or inability of an employee to state an idea or a set of facts clearly and concisely.

Most people work for institutions—businesses and banks, insurance firms and law firms, government agencies, school systems, nonprofit organizations and various other entities. Many of them are executives whose writing goes out to the public: the corporation president addressing his stockholders, the bank manager explaining a change in procedure, the school principal writing a newsletter to parents. Whoever they are, they are so uncomfortable or fearful that their sentences lack all humanity—and so do their institutions. In fact, it is hard to imagine that these are real places where real men and women come to work every morning.

But just because people work for an institution they don't have to write like one. Institutions can be warmed up. Administrators and executives can be turned into human beings. Information can be imparted clearly and without pompous verbosity. It's a question of remembering that readers identify with people, not with abstractions like "profitability," or with Latinate nouns like "utilization" and "implementation," or with passive-verb constructions in which nobody can be visualized doing something ("pre-feasibility studies are in the paperwork stage").

Nowhere has the point been made better than in George Orwell's "translation" into modern bureaucratic fuzz of this famous verse from Ecclesiastes:

> I returned and saw under the sun, that the race is not to the swift, nor the battle to the strong, neither yet bread to the wise, nor yet riches to men of understanding, nor yet favor to men of skill; but time and chance happeneth to them all.

Orwell's version goes:

> Objective consideration of contemporary phenomena compels the conclusion that success or failure in competitive activities exhibits no tendency to be commensurate with innate capacity, but that a considerable element of the unpredictable must invariably be taken into account.

Gone are the short words and vivid images from everyday life —the race and the battle, the bread and the riches—and in their place have waddled the long and flabby nouns of generalized meaning. Gone is any sense of what one person did ("I returned") or what he realized ("saw") about one of life's central mysteries: the capriciousness of fate.

I'll use school principals as my first example here, not because they are the worst offenders (they aren't), but because I happen to have such an example. My points are intended, however, for all the big and small executives in all the organizations where language has lost its humanity and nobody quite knows what the people in charge are trying to say.

My encounter with the principals began when I got a call from Ernest B. Fleishman, superintendent of schools in Greenwich, Conn. "We'd like you to come and 'dejargonize' us," he said. "We don't think we can teach students to write unless all of us at the top of the school system clean up our own writing." He said he would send me some typical materials that had originated within the system. His idea was for me to analyze the writing and then conduct a workshop.

What appealed to me was the willingness of Dr. Fleishman and his colleagues to make themselves vulnerable. We decided on a date, and soon a fat envelope arrived. It contained various internal memos and a number of mimeographed newsletters that had been mailed to parents by the sixteen elementary, junior and senior high schools ("A Message from the Principal").

The newsletters had a cheery and informal look. Obviously the system was making an effort to communicate warmly with its families. But even at first glance certain chilly phrases caught my eye—"prioritized evaluative procedures," "modified departmentalized schedule"—and one principal promised that his school would provide "enhanced positive learning environments." Just as obviously the system wasn't communicating as warmly as it thought it was.

I studied the principals' material and divided it into good and bad examples. On the appointed morning in Greenwich I found forty principals, directors and curriculum coordinators assembled and eager to learn. I said that I could only applaud them for submitting to a process that so threatened their identity. In the national clamor over why Johnny can't write, Dr. Fleishman was the first adult in my experience who admitted that youth has no monopoly on verbal sludge and that the problem must also be attacked at the top.

I told the principals that as parents we want to think of the men and women who run our children's schools as people not unlike ourselves. We are suspicious of pretentiousness, of all the fad words that the social scientists have coined to avoid the horrid necessity of making themselves clear to ordinary mortals. I urged them to be natural. How we write and how we talk is how we define ourselves.

I asked them to listen to how they were defining themselves to the community. I had made forty copies of certain bad examples, changing the names of the schools and principals. I explained that I would read some of the examples aloud. Later we would see if they could turn what they had written into plain English. This was my first example:

> Dear Parent:
> We have established a special phone communication system to provide additional opportunities for parent input. During this year we will give added emphasis to the goal of communication and utilize a variety of means to accomplish this goal. Your inputs, from the unique position as a parent, will help us to plan and implement an educational plan that meets the needs of your child. An open dialogue, feedback and sharing of information between parents and teachers will enable us to work with your child in the most effective manner.
>
> DR. GEORGE B. JONES
> Principal

That is the kind of communication I don't want to receive, unique though my parent inputs might be. I'd like to be told that the school is going to make it easier for me to telephone the teachers and that they hope I'll call often to discuss how my children are getting along. Instead the parent gets junk: "special phone communication system," "added emphasis to the goal of communication," "plan and implement an educational plan." As for "open dialogue, feedback and sharing of information," they are three ways of saying the same thing.

Dr. Jones is clearly a man who means well, and his plan is one that we all want: a chance to pick up the phone and tell the principal what a great kid Johnny is despite that unfortunate incident in the playground last Tuesday. But Dr. Jones doesn't sound like a person I want to call. In fact, he doesn't sound like a person. His message could have been tapped out by a computer. He is squandering a rich resource: himself.

Another example that I chose was a "Principal's Greeting" sent to parents at the start of the year. It consisted of two paragraphs that were very different:

> Fundamentally, Foster is a good school. Pupils who require help in certain subjects or study skills areas are receiving special attention. In the school year ahead we seek to provide enhanced positive learning environments. Children, and staff, must work in an atmosphere that is conducive to learning. Wide varieties of instructional materials are needed. Careful attention to individual abilities and learning styles is required. Co-operation between school and home is extremely important to the learning process. All of us should be aware of desired educational objectives for every child.

> Keep informed about what is planned for our children this year and let us know about your own questions and about any special needs your child may have. I have met many of you in the first few weeks. Please continue to stop in to introduce yourself or to talk about Foster. I look forward to a very productive year for all of us.

> Dr. Ray B. Dawson
> Principal

In the second paragraph I'm being greeted by a person; in the first I'm hearing from an educator. I like the real Dr. Dawson of Paragraph 2. He talks in warm and comfortable phrases: "Keep informed," "Let us know," "I have met," "Please continue," "I look forward."

By contrast, Educator Dawson of Paragraph 1 never uses "I" or even suggests a sense of "I." He falls back on the jargon of his profession, where he feels safe, not stopping to notice that he really isn't telling the parent anything. What are "study skills areas" and how do they differ from "subjects"? What are "enhanced positive learning environments" and how do they differ from "an atmosphere that is conducive to learning"? What are "wide varieties of instructional materials": pencils, textbooks, filmstrips? What exactly are "learning styles"? What "educational objectives" are "desired," and who desires them?

The second paragraph, in short, is warm and personal; the other is pedantic and vague. This was a pattern that I found repeatedly. Whenever the principals wrote to notify the parents of some human detail they wrote with humanity:

> It seems that traffic is beginning to pile up again in front of the school. If you can possibly do so, please come to the rear of the school for your child at the end of the day.

> I would appreciate it if you would speak with your children about their behavior in the cafeteria. Many of you would be totally dismayed if you could observe the manners of your children while they are eating. Check occasionally to see if they owe money for lunch. Sometimes children are very slow in repaying.

But when the educators wrote to explain how they proposed to do their educating, they vanished without a trace:

> In this document you will find the program goals and objectives that have been identified and prioritized. Evaluative procedures for the objectives were also established based on acceptable criteria.

> Prior to the implementation of the above practice, students were given very little exposure to multiple choice questions. It is felt that the use of practice questions correlated to the unit that a student is presently studying has had an extremely positive effect as the test scores confirm.

After I had read various good and bad examples, the principals began to hear the difference between their true selves and
their educator selves. The problem was how to close the gap.
I recited my articles of faith: humanity, clarity, simplicity, vitality. I explained about using active verbs and avoiding windy
nouns. I told them not to use the private vocabulary of education as a crutch. There is almost no specialized subject that can't
be made accessible in good English.

These were all basic tenets, but the principals wrote them
down as if they had never heard them before—and maybe they
hadn't, or at least not for many years. Perhaps this is why
bureaucratic prose becomes so turgid, whatever the bureau-
cracy. Once an administrator rises to a certain level, nobody
ever points out to him again the beauty of a short declarative
sentence, or shows him how his writing has become swollen
with ornate generalizations.

Finally our workshop got down to work. I distributed my
forty copies and asked the principals to rewrite the more knotty
sentences. It was a grim moment. They had met the enemy for
the first time. They scribbled on their pads and scratched out
what they had scribbled. Some didn't write anything. Some
crumpled their paper. They began, in fact, to look like writers.
An awful silence hung over the room, broken only by the crossing out of sentences and the crumpling of paper. They began
to sound like writers.

As the day went on, they slowly relaxed. They began to write
in the first person and to use active verbs. For a while they still
couldn't loose their grip on long words and vague nouns ("parent communication response"). But gradually their sentences
became human. When I asked them to tackle "Evaluative
procedures for the objectives were established based on acceptable criteria," one of them wrote: "At the end of the year we
will evaluate our progress." Another wrote: "We will see how
well we have succeeded."

That's the kind of plain talk that a parent wants. It's also what the stockholder wants from his corporation, what the customer wants from his bank, what the widow wants from the government office that is handling her social security. There is a yearning for human contact and a resentment of bombast. Any institution that won't take the trouble in its writing to be both clear and personal will lose friends, customers and money. Let me put it another way for business executives: a shortfall will be experienced in anticipated profitability.

Still, plain talk will not be easily achieved in corporate America. Too much vanity is on the line. Executives at every level are prisoners of the notion that a simple style reflects a simple mind. Actually a simple style is the result of hard work and hard thinking; a muddy style reflects a muddy thinker or a person too lazy to organize his thoughts.

I learned about corporate America by venturing out into it, after Greenwich, to conduct similar workshops for several of the country's biggest corporations, which also asked to be dejargonized. I worked with men and women who produce the vast amounts of written material that these huge companies generate for internal and external consumption.

The internal material consists of house organs and newsletters—daily, weekly and monthly—that are written to tell employees what is happening at their "facility" and to give them a sense of belonging. The external material includes the glossy magazines that go to the public, the speeches that are delivered by the president, and releases that are sent to the press. I found almost all of it lacking in human juices and much of it impenetrable.

Typical of the sentences in the newsletters were these:

> Included was the Configuration Requirements Processing (CRP) delivery containing the first complete process-control tables that will be used to specify software requirements by mission and the Software Checkout (SWCO)

confidence tape for validating the real-time Mission Control application programs.

Announced concurrently with the above enhancements were changes to the System Support Program, a program product which operates in conjunction with the NCP. Among the additional functional enhancements are dynamic reconfiguration and inter-systems communications.

There is no joy for the writer in such work, and certainly none for the reader. It is language out of *Star Trek,* and if I were an employee I would not be cheered—or informed—by these efforts to raise my morale. In fact, I would soon stop reading them, just as I soon learned not to try to decipher the internal memos that circulate through Yale. Life is too short for such dreary mental gymnastics.

I told the corporate writers that they had to find the people behind these fine scientific achievements. "Go to the engineer who created the system," I said, "or to the technicians who assembled it, and get them to tell you in their own words how the idea came to them, or how they put it together, and how it will be used." The way to warm up an institution is to locate the missing "I." He or she is the most interesting part of any story.

The writers explained that they often did interview the engineer but couldn't get him to talk English. They showed me some typical quotations in their newsletters that proved the point all too well. The engineers spoke in an arcane language studded with acronyms ("Sub-system support is available only with VSAG or TNA").

I said that the writers had to keep going back to the engineer until he finally made himself intelligible. They said that the engineer didn't *want* to be made intelligible: if he spoke too simply he would look like a jerk to his peers. I said that their responsibility was to the facts and to the reader, not to the vanity of the engineer. I urged them to believe in themselves as writers and not to relinquish control. They replied that this was easier said than done in hierarchical corporations where approval is required at various higher levels. I sensed an undercurrent of fear: do things the company way and don't risk your job trying to make the company human.

But I found that high executives were equally victimized by the syndrome of sounding important. One corporation, for instance, had a monthly newsletter to enable "management" to share its concerns with middle managers and lower employees. Prominent in every issue was a message of exhortation from the division vice-president, whom I'll call Vernon B. Smith. Judging by his monthly message, he was a pompous ass, saying nothing and saying it in inflated verbiage.

When I mentioned this, the writers said that Vernon B. Smith was actually a diffident man and a good executive with a good mind. They pointed out that he doesn't write the message himself; it's written for him. I said that Vernon B. Smith was being done a disservice—that the writers should go to him every month (with a tape recorder, if necessary) and stay there until he talked about his concerns in the same language that he would use when he got home and talked to Mrs. Vernon B. Smith.

What I realized—by extension—was that most executives in America don't write what appears over their signature or what they say in their speeches. They have surrendered the qualities that make them unique. If they and their institutions seem cold and pretentious it is because they acquiesce in the process of being pumped up and dried out. Preoccupied with their complex equipment, they forget that words are among the most powerful of all tools—for good and bad.

If you work for an institution, whatever your job, whatever your level, be yourself when you write. You will stand out as a real person among the robots, and your example might even persuade Vernon B. Smith to write his own stuff.

16. Sports

I learned about the circuit clout before I learned about the electrical circuit. I also learned early—as a child addict of the sports pages—that a hurler (or twirler) who faces left when he toes the slab is a southpaw or a portsider. Southpaws were always lanky, portsiders always chunky, though I have never heard "chunky" applied to anything else except peanut butter (to distinguish it from "creamy") and I have no idea what a chunky person would look like. When hurlers fired the old horsehide, a batsman would try to solve their slants. If he succeeded he might rap a sharp bingle to the outfield, garnering a win for the home contingent, or at least knotting the count. If not, he might bounce into a twin killing, snuffing out a rally and dimming his team's hopes in the flag scramble.

I could go on, mining every sport for its lingo and extracting from the mother lode a variety of words found nowhere else in the mother tongue. Do we ever "garner" anything except a win? I could write of hoopsters and pucksters, grapplers and matmen, strapping oarsmen and gridiron standouts. I could rhapsodize about the old pigskin—far more passionately than any pig farmer—or describe the frenzied bleacherites caught up in the excitement of the autumn classic. I could, in short, write in sports English instead of good English, as if they were two different languages. Of course they're not. As in the case of writing about science or any other special subject, there is no substitute for the best.

What, you might ask, is wrong with "southpaw"? Shouldn't we be grateful for the addition to our language of a word so picturesque? Why isn't it a relief to have twirlers and circuit clouts instead of the same old pitchers and home runs? The answer is that these words have become even cheaper currency than the coins they were meant to replace. They come flooding automatically out of the typewriter of every scribe (sports-writer) in every pressbox.

The man who first thought of "southpaw" had a right to be pleased. I like to think that he allowed himself the small smile that is the due of anyone who invents a good novelty. But how long ago was that? The color that "southpaw" added to the language has paled with decades of repetition, along with the hundreds of other idioms that now form the fabric of daily sportswriting. There is a weariness about them that leaves us numb. We read the articles to find out who won, and how, but we don't read them with any real enjoyment.

The best sportswriters know this. They avoid the exhausted synonyms and strive for freshness elsewhere in the construction of a sentence. You can search the columns of Red Smith and never find a batsman bouncing into a twin killing. Smith is not afraid to let a batter hit into a double play. But you will find hundreds of unusual words—good English words—chosen with precision and fitted into situations where no other sportswriter would put them. They gratify us because the writer obviously cares about using fresh imagery in a field where his competitors settle for the same old stuff. This is why Red Smith is still in business after more than fifty years of writing, and why his competitors have long since been sent—as they would be the first to say—to the showers.

Across the years I remember countless phrases in Red Smith's columns that took me by surprise with their humor and originality. It was a pleasure to read about a quarterback who was "scraped off the turf like apple butter." I remember countless times when Smith, a devout angler, baited his hook and came up with that slippery fish, a sports commissioner, gasping for air.

"In most professional sports the bottom has just about dropped out of the czar business," he wrote in 1971, noting once again that the cupidity of team owners has a tendency to outrun the courage of the sport's monitors. "The first and toughest of the overlords was Kenesaw Mountain Landis, who came to power in 1920 and ruled with a heavy hand until his death in 1944. But if baseball started with Little Caesar, it wound up with Ethelred the Unready." Red Smith is the daily guardian of our perspective, a writer who keeps us honest. But this is largely because he is writing good English. His style is not only graceful but strong enough to carry strong convictions.

What keeps the average sportswriter from writing good English is, first, the misapprehension that he shouldn't be trying to. He has been reared on so much jargon, so many clichés, that he thinks they are the required tools of the trade.

He is also obsessed by synonyms. He has a dread of repeating the word that is easiest for the reader to visualize—batter, runner, golfer, boxer—if a synonym can be found. And usually, with exertion, it can. This excerpt from a college newspaper is typical:

> Bob Hornsby extended his skein yesterday by toppling Dartmouth's Jerry Smithers, 6–4, 6–2, to lead the netmen to victory over a surprisingly strong foe. The gangling junior put his big serve to good use in keeping the Green captain off balance. The Memphis native was in top form as he racked up the first four games, breaking the Indian's service twice in the first four games. The Exeter graduate faltered and the Hanover mainstay rallied to cop three games. But the racquet ace was not to be denied, and Smithers' attempt to knot the first stanza at 4–4 failed when

he was passed by a cross-court volley on the sixth deuce
point. The redhead was simply too determined, and . . .

Whatever became of Bob Hornsby? Well might you ask.
Hornsby has been metamorphosed within one paragraph into
the gangling junior, the Memphis native, the Exeter graduate,
the racquet ace and the redhead. The reader doesn't know him
in these various disguises—or care. He only wants the clearest
picture of what happened. Never be afraid to repeat the
player's name and to keep the details of the game simple. A set
or an inning doesn't have to be recycled into a stanza or a frame
just to avoid redundancy. The cure is worse than the ailment.

Another obsession is with numbers. True, every sports addict
lives with a head full of statistics, cross-filed for ready access, and
many a baseball fan who once flunked simple arithmetic can
perform prodigies of instant calculation in the ball park on a
summer afternoon. Still, some statistics are more important
than others. If a pitcher wins his twentieth game, if a golfer
shoots a 61, if a runner runs the mile in 3:48, please mention it.
But don't get carried away:

> AUBURN, Ala., Nov. 1 (UPI)—Pat Sullivan, Auburn's soph-
> omore quarterback, scored two touchdowns and passed for
> two today to hand Florida a 38–12 defeat, the first of the
> season for the ninth-ranked Gators.
>
> John Reaves of Florida broke two Southeastern Confer-
> ence records and tied another. The tall sophomore from
> Tampa, Fla., gained 369 yards passing, pushing his six-
> game season total to 2,115. That broke the S.E.C. season
> record of 2,012 set by the 1966 Heisman trophy winner, in
> 10 games.
>
> Reaves attempted 66 passes—an S.E.C. record—and tied
> the record of 33 completions set this fall by Mississippi's
> Archie Manning.
>
> Fortunately for Auburn, nine of Reaves's passes were
> intercepted—breaking the S.E.C. record of eight intercep-

tions suffered by Georgia's Zeke Bratkowski against Georgia Tech in 1951.

Reaves's performance left him only a few yards short of the S.E.C. season total offense record of 2,187 set by Georgia's Frank Sinkwich in 11 games in 1942. And his two touchdown passes against Auburn left him only one touchdown pass short of the S.E.C. season record of 23 set in 1950 by Kentucky's Babe Parilli. . . .

Those are the first five paragraphs of a six-paragraph story that was prominently displayed in my New York newspaper, a long way from Auburn. It has a certain mounting hilarity—a figure freak amok at his typewriter. But can anybody read it? And does anybody care? Only Zeke Bratkowski—finally off the hook.

Sports is one of the richest fields now open to the nonfiction writer. Many authors better known for "serious" books have done some of their most solid work as observers of athletic combat. John McPhee's *Levels of the Game* and George Plimpton's *Paper Lion*—one a book about tennis, the other about professional football—take us deeply into the lives of the players. In mere detail they have enough information to keep any fan happy. But what makes them special is their humanity. Who is this strange bird—the winning athlete—and what mysterious engines keep him going?

One of the classics in the literature of baseball is John Updike's account of Ted Williams' final game, on September 28, 1960. The article builds to the almost mythical moment in the eighth inning when the forty-two-year-old "Kid," coming up for his last time at bat in Fenway Park, hits one over the wall. But before that Updike has compressed much of the career of "this brittle and temperamental player" in one paragraph that is as graceful as Williams' own swing:

I remember watching one of his home runs from the bleachers of Shibe Park; it went over the first baseman's head and rose meticulously along a straight line and was still rising when it cleared the fence. The trajectory seemed qualitatively different from anything anyone else might hit. For me, Williams is the classic ballplayer of the game on a hot August weekday, before a small crowd, when the only thing at stake is the tissue-thin difference between a thing done well and a thing done ill. Baseball is a game of the long season, of relentless and gradual averaging-out. Irrelevance —since the reference point of most individual games is remote and statistical—always threatens its interest, which can be maintained not by the occasional heroics that sports-writers feed upon but by players who always care; who care, that is to say, about themselves and their art. Insofar as the clutch hitter is not a sportswriter's myth, he is a vulgarity, like a writer who writes only for money. It may be that, compared to managers' dreams, such as Joe Di-Maggio and the always helpful Stan Musial, Williams is an icy star. But of all team sports, baseball, with its graceful intermittences of action, its immense and tranquil field sparsely settled with poised men in white, its dispassionate mathematics, seems to me best suited to accommodate, and be ornamented by, a loner. It is essentially a lonely game. No other player visible to my generation has concen-trated within himself so much of the sport's poignance, has so assiduously refined his natural skills, has so constantly brought to the plate that intensity of competence that crowds the throat with joy.

From the "sparsely settled" diamond to the densely popu-lated chessboard may seem an unlikely leap. But to a good writer there is always the central mystery of a game's fascina-tion for the player, whatever the game. George Steiner's *Fields of Force,* an account of the Fischer-Spassky chess championship and of past title matches and champions, is a masterpiece of sports reporting, taking the reader into terrain more dizzying than any bobsled run:

> Whatever Fischer's idiosyncrasies, there are abundant impulses to paranoia and unreality in chess itself, in the violence and autistic passion of the game. Like the inner workings of mathematics and music, these qualities are next to impossible to communicate in words. . . .
>
> [But] something of the full horror and harmony of the abysmal depths, of the lunatic magic of endless vertigo, can be expressed numerically. The first four moves can lead to 70,000 different positions. The number of possible ways of playing the first ten moves on each side is such that if every man, woman and child on the earth played without respite it would require more than 217 billion years to go through them all. The most recent estimate of the number of different games that can be played is of the order of 25×10^{115}, a product fantastically larger than the generally assumed sum of atoms in the universe. This does not mean that identical *positions* will not turn up. Openings will often run the same course, and an end-game problem set by al-Adli in an Arab manuscript of the ninth century came up in actual play in 1945 (Jorgensen-Sorensen). But the odds against a duplication of a major portion of a game are far more than astronomical. In brief, as far as we can look ahead to a future for the species and this galaxy the variety of play in chess remains inexhaustible.

Good sportswriting has crossed over into whole new realms, undreamed of by the hacks who still sit in the pressbox reporting the stellar exploits of chunky portsiders and Ruthian sluggers. It's one of the richest frontiers, incidentally, for women writers. Even Ruth has been ushered down from the sanitized slopes of Olympus and converted into a real person, with appetites as big as his girth, in Robert W. Creamer's fine biography, *Babe*. "The legend comes alive," says the book's subtitle, which is certainly what Ruth would have wanted, hard though some of the facts may be on those who would like him to stay legendary.

This is only one of many realities that have come crowding into what was until recently a simple fairyland world. Just to process the daily medical news, for instance, is no easy task for the modern fan—matters of fitness, injury and orthopedic disarray. Hardly a man is now alive who can't draw a transverse section of the human knee after surgery, or digress on bone chips and rotator disks in a pitcher's arm.

Another new element is high finance. In the few years since baseball's hired hands were legally sprung from bondage and allowed to peddle themselves to the highest bidder, I have often opened the sports section and thought that I had stumbled into the business pages by mistake. Million-dollar contracts of infinite complexity swim before my eyes, replete with deferred payments, bonuses and annuities, some extending beyond the year 2000.

Big money in turn has brought big emotional trouble. Envy is the new worm in the apple of sport. To read about the New York Yankees as they bickered through the summer of 1977, when Reggie Jackson had arrived toting his monetary bundle, was like reading Ann Landers. The game was secondary; first we had to learn whose feelings were hurt, whose pride was wounded. In once-sedate tennis, the pot of gold is now enormous and the players are strung as tightly as their racquets. In football and basketball the pay is sky-high, and so is the umbrage.

"It wasn't my idea for basketball to become tax-shelter show biz," Bill Bradley writes in *Life on the Run*, a chronicle of his seasons with the New York Knicks. Bradley's book is one of the best examples of the new sportswriting because it ponders the darker forces that are altering the quality of American sport— the greed of entrepreneurs, the blind worship of stars, the inability to accept defeat:

After Van's departure I realized that no matter how kind, friendly and genuinely interested the owners may be, in the end most players are little more than depreciable assets to them.

Self-definition comes from external sources, not from within. While their physical skill lasts, professional athletes are celebrities—fondled and excused, praised and believed. Only toward the end of their careers do the stars realize that their sense of identity is insufficient.

The winning team, like the conquering army, claims everything in its path and seems to say that only winning is important. Yet victory has very narrow meanings and can become a destructive force. The taste of defeat has a richness of experience all its own.

Bradley's book is also an excellent travel journal, catching the fatigue and loneliness of the professional athlete's nomadic life —the countless night flights and bus rides, the dreary days and endless waits in motel rooms and terminals:

In the airports that have become our commuter stations we see so many dramatic personal moments that we are calloused. To some, we live romantic lives. To me, every day is a struggle to stay in touch with life's subtleties.

American sport has always been interwoven with social history, and the best sportswriters are those who will make the connection. A small but pleasant example of making the connection was a small but pleasant piece by Jean Shepherd about the Indianapolis 500. The article, which ran in the Sunday sports section of the *New York Times,* explains that the Indy has only one counterpart in American sport—the Kentucky Derby —and that both "can only be understood by the outsider in terms of folklore":

Any horse that wins the Derby enters the pearly gates of history forever. Hundreds of horses have won "classics" over the years, but even non-horseplayers remember Derby winners. So it is with the 500. Who knows or cares what other races Wilbur Shaw might have won in his great career? The fact that he took the 500 three times makes him immortal.

Why the Derby when there are other, richer races? A little history helps. Kentucky, with its great plantations, its soft rolling hills and lazy summers, was the true horse country of America, and 100 years ago when the Derby was born it pitted one aristocratic horse against the other. It was not just another race, but something that came out of the air and the land and the people who lived on it. . . .

Indiana in the early days was to the automobile as Kentucky was and is to the horse. Some of the truly great machines by any world standard were born and bred on the Indiana flatlands. The stylish and terrifying Dusenbergs created by the almost mythical Dusenberg brothers, Fred and August, were hammered out a few miles from the brick track. The Auburn, the Cord and the great racing Studebakers were all spawned in dusty Indiana hamlets and came together every spring in the dawn of automobiling to battle it out.

The automobile also means much more to the common people of the great plains than it does to the city folk who huddle jammed together in the great urban East. It meant, and still means, freedom, mobility and, above all, a way out for lives that are often as monotonous as the landscape they are lived in.

These are the values to look for when you write about sport —people, places, the link between past and present, the tug of the future. Observe closely. Hang around the track and the paddock, the ball park and the rink. Interview in depth. Listen to old-timers. Ponder the changes. Write well.

17. Criticism

Every writer wants at some time to be a critic. The small-town reporter dreams of the moment when his editor will summon him to cover the Russian ballet troupe, the concert pianist, the touring repertory company that has been booked into the local auditorium. Then he will trot out all the hard-won words of his college education—"intuit" and "sensibility" and "Kafka-esque"—and show the whole county that he knows a *glissando* from an *entrechat*. He will discern more symbolism in Ibsen than Ibsen ever thought of.

This is part of the urge. Criticism is the stage on which journalists do their fanciest strutting.

It is also where reputations for wit are born. The American vernacular is rich in epigrams ("She ran the gamut of emotions from A to B") minted by people like Dorothy Parker and George S. Kaufman who became famous partly by minting them, and the temptation to make an instant name at the expense of some talentless ham is too strong for all but the most saintly.

Not that the epigrams aren't enjoyable. I particularly like Kaufman's hint that Raymond Massey in *Abe Lincoln in Illinois* was perhaps overplaying the title role: "Massey won't be satisfied until he's assassinated." But true wit is rare, and a thousand barbed arrows fall at the feet of the archer for every one

that flies. It is also too facile an approach if you want to write
serious criticism, for, by no accident, the only epigrams that
have survived are cruel ones. It is far easier to bury Caesar than
to praise him—and that goes for Cleopatra, too. But to say why
you think that a play is *good,* in words that don't sound banal,
is one of the hardest chores in the business.

So don't be deluded that criticism is an easy route to glory.
Nor does the job carry as much power as is widely supposed.
Probably only the daily drama critic of the *New York Times* can
make or break the product—a new play—and a music critic has
almost no power at all, writing, as he does, about a cluster of
sounds that have vanished into the air and will never be heard
in quite the same way again.

As for literary critics, they have never kept the best-seller list
from becoming a nesting-ground for authors like Harold Robbins and Irving Wallace—whose sensibility they don't intuit—
and movie critics, the most pretentious of the lot, wield almost
no influence except in the case of a foreign film, where a good
review can lengthen its run. You only have to compare the
critics' appraisal and the box-office receipts of, say, *The Poseidon
Adventure* to see the process of non-influence in full flower. The
critics judged it in artistic terms and declared it junk. But the
film wasn't conceived in artistic terms—it was a movie about an
ocean liner that turns upside down. It was junk, but entertaining junk.

A distinction should therefore be made between a "critic"
and a "reviewer." In general a reviewer writes for a newspaper or a popular magazine, and what he covers is not primarily an art but an industry—the output of, for instance,
the television industry, the motion-picture industry and, increasingly, the publishing industry in its outpouring of "gift
books," cookbooks, how-to books, sex books and other such
items of merchandise.

As a reviewer your job is more to report than to make an
aesthetic judgment. You are the deputy for the average man or

woman who wants to know: "What is the new TV series about?" "Is the movie too dirty for the kids?" "Will the book really improve my sex life or tell me how to make a chocolate mousse?" Think what *you* would want to know if *you* had to spend the money for the movie, the baby-sitter and the long-promised dinner at a good restaurant. Obviously you will make your review simpler and less sophisticated than if you were criticizing a new novel by Thomas Pynchon.

And yet I suggest several conditions that apply equally to good reviewing and good criticism.

One is that a critic should like—or, better still, love—the medium that he is reviewing. If you think movies are dumb, don't write about them. The reader deserves a lifelong movie buff who will bring with him a reservoir of knowledge, passion and prejudice. I don't mean that the critic has to like every film. On the contrary, his prejudices are as important as his passions —criticism is, after all, only one person's opinion and a highly subjective form. But he should go to every movie wanting to like it. If he is more often disappointed than pleased, it is because the film has failed to live up to what he knows are its best possibilities. This is far different from the critic who prides himself on hating everything, who relishes giving us his weekly dose of bile. He becomes tiresome faster than you can say "Kafkaesque."

Another rule is: don't give away too much of the plot. Tell the reader just enough to let him decide whether it's the kind of story that he tends to enjoy, but not so much that you will kill his eventual enjoyment. One sentence will often do the trick. "This is a picture about a whimsical Irish priest who enlists the help of three orphan boys dressed as leprechauns to haunt a village where a mean widow has hidden a crock of gold coins." I couldn't be flailed into seeing that movie—I've had my fill of "the little people" on stage and screen. But there are legions who don't share that particular crotchet of mine and would flock to the film. Don't spoil their pleasure by revealing every twist of the narrative—especially the funny part about the troll under the bridge.

A third principle is to use as much specific detail as possible. This avoids dealing in generalities, which, being generalities, mean nothing. "The play is always fascinating" is a typical critic's sentence. But *how* is it fascinating? Your idea of fascinating is different from the reader's. Cite a few examples and let him weigh them on his own fascination scale. Here are excerpts from two separate reviews of a film directed by Joseph Losey. (1) "In its attempts to be civilized and restrained it denies its possibilities for vulgarity and mistakes bloodlessness for taste." The sentence is vague, giving us at the most a whiff of the movie's mood but no image that we can visualize. (2) "Losey pursues a style that finds portents in lampshades and meanings in table settings." The sentence is precise—we know just what kind of arty film-making this is. We can almost see the camera lingering with studied sluggishness over the family crystal.

In book reviewing this means allowing the author's words to do their own documentation. Don't say, for instance, that Tom Wolfe's style is gaudy and unusual. Quote a few of his gaudy and unusual sentences and let the reader see how distinctive they are, how quirky. In reviewing a play, don't just tell us that the set is "striking." Describe its various levels, or how it is ingeniously lit, or how it helps the actors to make their entrances and exits as a less imaginative set would not. Put the reader in your theater seat. Help him to see what you saw.

A final caution is to avoid the ecstatic adjectives that occupy such disproportionate space in every critic's quiver—words like "enthralling" and "luminous." Good criticism needs a lean and vivid style to express what you observed and what you think. Florid adjectives smack of the panting prose with which *Vogue* likes to disclose its latest chichi discovery: "We've just heard about the most utterly enchanting little beach at Cozumel."

So much for reviewing and the simpler rules of the game. What, then, is criticism?

Criticism is a serious intellectual act. It tries to appraise serious works of art and to place them in the context of what has
been done before in that medium or by that particular artist.
This doesn't mean that the critic must limit himself to the work
of men and women whose aims are high; he may select some
commercial product like *All in the Family* to make a point
about American taste and values. But on the whole he doesn't
want to waste his time on peddlers. He sees himself as a scholar,
and what interests him is the play of ideas in his field.

Therefore if you want to be a critic, steep yourself in the
literature of the medium that you hope to make your province.
If your goal is to be a theater critic, see every possible play—
the good and the bad, the old and the new. Catch up on the past
by reading the classics or seeing them in revival. Know your
Shakespeare and Shaw, your Chekhov and Molière, your Arthur
Miller and Tennessee Williams, and know what they meant to
audiences of their era and how they broke new ground. Know
the history of the American musical: the distinctive contribution of Jerome Kern and the Gershwin brothers, of Cole Porter,
of Rodgers and Hart and Hammerstein, of Frank Loesser and
Stephen Sondheim, of Agnes De Mille and Jerome Robbins.
Learn everything you can about the great actors and directors
and how their methods differed, and about the great clowns like
Bert Lahr. Only then can you place every new drama within an
older tradition, recognize genius when it comes along and tell
the pioneer from the imitator.

I could make the same kind of list for every art. A film critic
who reviews a new Fellini picture without having seen most of
Fellini's earlier films is not much help to the serious movie-goer.
A music critic should know not only his Bach and Palestrina, his
Mozart and Beethoven, but his Schoenberg and Satie, his Ives
and Varèse—the theoreticians and mavericks and electronic
experimenters.

Obviously I am now also assuming a more urbane body of
readers. As a critic you can presuppose certain shared areas of

knowledge with the men and women you are writing for. You
don't have to tell them that William Faulkner was a Southern
novelist. What you *do* have to do, if you are assessing the first
novel of a Southern author and weighing Faulkner's influence,
is to generate a provocative idea and to throw it onto the page
where your fellow scholars can savor it. They may disagree with
your point—that's part of their intellectual fun. But at least they
have enjoyed the turn of your mind and the journey that took
you to your conclusion. We like a good critic as much for his
personality as for his opinions.

Let me take you journeying with a great film critic, James
Agee, as he reveals what he liked best about Laurence Olivier's
Henry V.

Some people, using I wonder what kind of dry ice for
comfort, insist that *Henry V* is relatively uninteresting
Shakespeare. [But] after hearing it, in this production, I
find it as hard to judge fairly even the best writing since
Shakespeare as it is to see the objects in a room after looking into the sun.

The one great glory of the film is this language. The
greatest credit I can assign to those who made the film is
that they have loved and served the language so well. I
don't feel that much of the delivery is inspired; it is merely
so good, so right, that the words set loose in the graciously
designed world of the screen, like so many uncaged birds,
fully enjoy and take care of themselves. Neither of the
grimmest Shakespearean vices is indulged: none of the text
is read in that human, down-to-earth, poetry-is-only-
hopped-up-prose manner which is doubtless only proper
when a charter subscriber to *PM* reads the [Max] Lerner
editorial to his shop-wise fellow traveler; nor is any of it
intoned in the nobler manner, as if by a spoiled deacon
celebrating the Black Mass down a section of sewerpipe.
Most of it is merely spoken by people who know and love

poetry as poetry and have spent a lifetime learning how to speak it accordingly. Their voices, faces and bodies are all in the charge of a man who has selected them as shrewdly as a good orchestrator selects and blends his instruments; and he combines and directs them as a good conductor conducts an orchestral piece. It is, in fact, no surprise to learn that Mr. Olivier is fond of music. Charming as it is to look at, the film is essentially less visual than musical.

Most of us remember *Henry V* for its beauty, its color, its robust vitality. Agee reminds us that it was built on still sturdier pillars. He also tells us a great deal about himself. How could we not take pleasure in a mind both so finely tuned to poetry and so impatient with the grandiose?

Turning to another medium, but to a mind no less original, here is an excerpt from *Living-Room War* by Michael J. Arlen. The book is a collection of the critical columns on television that Arlen wrote for *The New Yorker* during 1966–67.

Vietnam is often referred to as "television's war," in the sense that this is the first war that has been brought to the people preponderantly by television. People indeed look at television. They really look at it. They look at Dick Van Dyke and become his friend. They look at thoughtful Chet Huntley and find him thoughtful, and at witty David Brinkley and find him witty. They look at Vietnam. They look at Vietnam, it seems, as a child kneeling in the corridor, his eye to the keyhole, looks at two grownups arguing in a locked room—the aperture of the keyhole small; the figures shadowy, mostly out of sight; the voices indistinct, isolated threats without meaning; isolated glimpses, part of an elbow, a man's jacket (who is the man?), part of a face, a woman's face. Ah, she is crying. One sees the tears. (The voices continue indistinctly.) One counts the tears. Two tears. Three tears. Two bombing raids. Four seek-and-destroy missions. Six administration pronouncements. Such a fine-looking woman. One searches in vain for the other grownup, but, ah, the keyhole is so small, he is somewhere never in the line of sight. Look! There is General Ky. Look! There are some planes returning safely to the *Ticonderoga.* I wonder (sometimes) what it is that the people who run television think about the war, because *they* have given us this keyhole view; we have given them the airwaves, and now, at this crucial time, they have given back to us this keyhole view—and I wonder if they truly think that those isolated glimpses of elbow, face, a swirl of dress (who *is* that other person anyway?) are all that we children can stand to see of what is going on inside the room.

This is criticism at its best: stylish, allusive, disturbing. It disturbs us—as criticism often should—because it jogs a firmly held set of beliefs and forces us to re-examine them. What holds our attention here is the metaphor of the keyhole, so exact and yet so mysterious. But what remains is a fundamental question about how a country's most powerful medium was telling the country's people about the war that they were fighting—and escalating. The column ran in 1966, when most Americans still supported the Vietnam war. Would they have turned against it sooner if TV had widened the keyhole, had shown us not only the "swirl of dress" but the severed head and the burning child? It is too late now to know. But at least one critic was keeping watch. Critics should always be among the first to notify us when the truths that we hold to be self-evident cease to be true.

Some arts, of course, are harder to catch in print than others. One is dance, which consists of movement. How can a writer freeze all the graceful leaps and pirouettes? Another is music. It is an art that we receive through our ears, yet the writer is stuck with describing it in words that we will see. At best he can only partly succeed, and many a music critic has built a long career by hiding from his readers behind a hedge of Italian technical terms. He will find just a shade too much *rubato* in a pianist, a tinge of shrillness in a soprano's *tessitura*.

But even in this world of evanescent notes a good critic can make sense of what happened by writing good English and by using references that mere mortals can understand. Virgil Thomson, whose columns ran in the *New York Herald Tribune* from 1940 to 1954, was an elegant practitioner. A composer himself, an erudite and cultivated man, he still never forgot that his readers were real people, and he wrote with a zest that swept them along, his style alive with pleasant surprises. He also never forgot that musicians are real people, and he didn't hesitate to shrink the giants to human scale. What other critic would dare to secularize the sainted Toscanini?

It is extraordinary how little musicians discuss among themselves Toscanini's rightness or wrongness about matters of speed and rhythm and the tonal amenities. Like other musicians, he is frequently apt about these and as frequently in error. What seems to be more important is his unvarying ability to put over a piece. He quite shamelessly whips up the tempo and sacrifices clarity and ignores a basic rhythm, just making the music, like his baton, go round and round, if he finds his audience's attention tending to waver. No piece has to mean anything specific; every piece has to provoke from its hearers a spontaneous vote of acceptance. This is what I call the "wow technique."

No *rubatos* or *tessituras* there, and no blind hero-worship. Yet the paragraph catches the essence of what made Toscanini great—an extra helping of showbiz. If his worshipers are offended to think that the essence contained so coarse an ingredient, they can continue to admire the Maestro for his "lyrical colorations" or "orchestral *tuttis*." I'll go along with Thomson's diagnosis, and so, I suspect, would the Maestro.

Here's another column by Virgil Thomson (a lead paragraph) which beguiles us instantly with its civility and charm:

One has known New York men who always had their suits made in Boston and elderly ladies from various parts of the Eastern seaboard who would never go anywhere else for a hat. Certainly we do not produce here [in New York] or import from any other provincial center such perfect musical tailoring as that which the Boston Symphony Orchestra exhibits for us in Carnegie Hall ten times a season and which was again displayed yesterday afternoon.

Finally, here is Thomson analyzing pure musicianship, telling us why a piano recital by Josef Lhevinne was not only perfect in itself but significantly better than the work of other major artists:

Any authoritative execution derives as much of its excellence from what the artist does not do as from what he does. If he doesn't do anything off color at all, he is correctly said to have taste. Mr. Lhevinne's taste is as authoritative as his technical method. Not one sectarian interpretation, not one personal fancy, not one stroke below the belt, not a sliver of ham, mars the universal acceptability of his readings. Everything he does is right and clear and complete. Everything he doesn't do is the whole list of all the things that mar the musical executions of lesser men.

All but one of these snippets from Agee, Arlen and Thomson were snipped from the middle of longer columns. They therefore don't demonstrate how a piece of good criticism should start. Here again you must orient the reader to the specialized world that he is about to enter. Even if he is a broadly educated person he needs to be told or reminded of certain facts. You can't just throw him into the water and expect him to swim easily. The water needs some warming up.

Notice how the following review of *Virginia Woolf,* a biography by Quentin Bell—from the *New York Times Book Review* —begins by summarizing the main details that we should know about Mrs. Woolf, about her paradoxical position in the world of letters, about her biographer and about her girlhood. Not until we possess this general information are we ready or interested enough to follow the critic, Michael Rosenthal, down more specific and scholarly paths.

Generally regarded as a genius by those who knew her, Virginia Woolf has long suffered from both the uncritical adulation and the virulent antipathy that genius frequently inspires. Lost in the conflict between those who worship at the altar of her sensitivity and those who decry her as snobbish, desiccated and irrelevant is any substantial notion of who Virginia Woolf actually was. Quentin Bell brings an impressive set of intellectual and genetic credentials to the task of unraveling the enigma of the "high priestess of Bloomsbury." As the son of Clive and Vanessa Bell and the nephew of Virginia, Bell would seem to be the most qualified person to reveal the facts of her life. An art critic of as much substance but less influence than his father, he has previously written a slim volume evaluating the Bloomsbury circle in which he grew up, and it was no surprise that Leonard Woolf, Virginia's husband, should have encouraged Bell to undertake the authorized biography. The results are in many ways startling.

The stage is well set. The final word, "startling," compels us to go on. How is the book startling?

Born in 1882, Virginia was the third of four children that Julia Duckworth Stephen, a young widow with three children of her own, presented Sir Leslie Stephen, the eminent Victorian whose sober rationalism and incessant self-pitying are immortalized in Mr. Ramsay of *To the Lighthouse.* The Stephen household was in fact very much like the Ramsays'; nourished by the warmth and compassion of their mother, the seven children regarded the austere Sir

Leslie with proper Victorian respect. But although there
were certain emotional disadvantages in having for a father
the man who in addition to editing the monumental *Dictionary of National Biography* managed to produce 15 assorted volumes of history, biography and criticism and well
over 100 long articles, there were a number of benefits as
well. Virginia grew up in an atmosphere densely packed
with words, ideas and, above all, books. . . .

It sounds normal enough—a respectable upper-middle-class
Victorian brood "clothed in the mantle of propriety," as the
critic puts it. "But no future study of Virginia Woolf will ever
be able to look at her life in quite the same way," he continues,
and we are off into the unwrapping of layers of lurking madness
and sexual exploration, without which, it now seems, no respectable upper-middle-class Victorian family was complete.
By the end of the review we see how the author's public art and
private suffering were intertwined from her childhood on, and
why suicide was the inevitable end of both. But we had to begin
with a plain set of facts.

Today criticism has many first cousins in journalism: the
newspaper or magazine column, the essay, the editorial, and
the essay-review, in which a critic digresses from a particular
book or cultural phenomenon into a larger point. (Gore Vidal
and Wilfrid Sheed have brought this form to a high polish.)
Many of the same principles that govern good criticism go into
these columns. A political columnist, for instance, must love
politics and know its ancient, tangled threads.

But what is common to all the forms is that they consist of
personal opinion. Even the editorial that uses "we" was obviously written by an "I." And what is crucial for you as the writer
is to express your opinion firmly. Don't cancel its strength with
last-minute evasions and escapes. The most boring sentence in
the daily newspaper is the last sentence of the editorial, which
says that "it is still too early to tell whether the new policy will

work" or that "the effectiveness of the decision remains to be seen." If it is still too early to tell, don't bother us with it at all, and as for what remains to be seen, *everything* remains to be seen, including what you will do ten minutes from now. Take your stand with conviction.

Many years ago when I was writing editorials for the *New York Herald Tribune,* the editor of the page was a huge and ungainly man from Texas. I respected him because he had no pretense and because he hated any undue circling around a subject. Every morning we would all discuss what editorials we would like to write for the next day and what position we would take. Frequently we weren't quite sure, especially the writer who was an expert on Latin America.

"What about that coup in Uruguay?" the editor would ask.

"It could represent progress for the economy," the writer would reply, "or then again it might destabilize the whole political situation. I suppose I could mention the possible benefits and then. . ."

"Well," the man from Texas would break in, "let's not go peeing down both legs."

It was a plea that he made often, and it was perhaps the most inelegant advice I ever received. But over a long career of writing reviews and columns and trying to make a point that I felt strongly about, it was also probably the best.

18. Humor

Humor is the secret weapon of the nonfiction writer. It is secret because so few writers realize that it is often their best tool—and sometimes their only tool—for making an important point.

If this strikes you as a paradox, you are not alone. The professional writer of humor lives with the knowledge that half of his readers never know what he is trying to do. I remember a reporter calling to ask how I happened to write a certain parody in *Life*. At the end he said, "Should I refer to you as a humorist? Or have you also written anything serious?"

The answer, of course, is that if you're trying to write humor almost everything that you do is serious. Few Americans understand this. We dismiss our humorists as triflers because they have never settled down to "real" work. So the Pulitzer Prizes go to authors like Ernest Hemingway and William Faulkner who are (God knows) serious and are therefore certified as men of literature. The prize has never gone to people like George Ade, H. L. Mencken, Ring Lardner, Robert Benchley, S. J. Perelman, Art Buchwald, Jules Feiffer and Woody Allen, who seem to be just fooling around.

They're not just fooling around. They are as serious in purpose as Hemingway or Faulkner—in fact, a national asset in forcing the country to see itself clearly. To them humor is urgent work. It's an attempt to say important things in a special way that regular writers aren't getting said in a regular way—or, if they are, it's so regular that nobody is reading it.

One cartoon by Herblock or Bill Mauldin is worth a hundred solemn editorials. One *Doonesbury* comic strip by Garry Trudeau—on journalism's exploitation of the "Son of Sam" killings, or on the tendency of voters to re-elect convicted Congressmen—is worth a thousand words of moralizing. One pop art painting of our neon landscape is worth a hundred earnest pieces deploring urban sprawl. It takes us by surprise and says "Look again!"

One *Catch-22* or *Dr. Strangelove* is more powerful than all the books and movies that try to show war "as it is." They are two works of comic imagination, but they are still the standard points of reference for anyone trying to warn us about the military mentality that could blow us all up tomorrow. Joseph Heller and Stanley Kubrick heightened the truth about war just enough to catch its essential lunacy, and we recognize it as lunacy. The joke is no joke.

This heightening of some crazy truth—to a level where it will be seen as crazy—is at the heart of what the serious humorist is trying to do. I'll give you an example that may help to explain how he goes about his mysterious work.

One day in the early 1960s I realized that suddenly half the girls and women in America were wearing haircurlers. It was of course an incredible new blight, and it was puzzling because I couldn't imagine when the girls took the curlers out. There was no evidence that they ever did. They wore them to the supermarket and to the movies and to church, and on dates, and quite possibly to their own weddings, and to many other places where they would be seen by many people. So what was the wonderful event for which they were saving the wonderful hairdo that would result from wearing all these wires?

I tried for a year to think of a way to write about this phenomenon—to make some comment that wouldn't sound pompous. I could have come right out and said "It's an outrage," "It's a national disgrace" and "Have these women no pride?" But that would have been a sermon, and sermons are the death of humor. The writer must find some comic device—satire, parody, irony, lampoon, nonsense—that he can use to disguise his serious point. Very often he never finds it, because it's hard to find, and the point doesn't get made.

Luckily, in this case my vigil was at last rewarded. I was browsing at my local newstand and saw four magazines side by side: *Hairdo, Celebrity Hairdo, Combout* and *Pouf.* I bought all four—to the alarm of my news dealer—and found that there exists a whole thriving world of journalism devoted solely to hair: life from the neck up, but not including the brain. The magazines had hundreds of diagrams of elaborate roller positions, and they also had lengthy columns in which a girl could send her roller problem to the editors for their advice. This was what I had needed. I invented a magazine called *Haircurl* and wrote a series of parody letters and replies. The piece ran in *Life* and it began like this:

Dear Haircurl:
I am 15 and am considered pretty in my group. I wear baby pink rollers, jumbo size. I have been going steady with a certain boy for 2 1/2 years and he has never seen me without my rollers. The other night I took them off and we had a terrible fight. "Your head looks small," he told me. He called me a dwarf and said I had misled him. How can I win him back?

HEARTSICK
Speonk, N.Y.

Dear Heartsick:
You have only yourself to blame for doing something so stupid. The latest "Haircurl" survey shows that 94% of

American girls now wear rollers in their hair 21.6 hours a day and 359 days a year. You tried to be different and you lost your fella. Take our advice and get some super-jumbo rollers (they come in your favorite baby pink shade, too) and your head will look bigger than ever and twice as lovely. Don't ever take them off again.

Dear Haircurl:

My problem is an intimate one, but I'm so upset that I just have to ask your advice. My boyfriend likes to run his fingers through my hair. The trouble is he keeps getting them pinched in my rollers. The other night a terribly embarrassing episode happened. We were at the movies and somehow my boyfriend got two of his fingers caught (it was right where the medium roller meets the clip-curl) and couldn't get them out. I felt very conspicuous leaving the theater with his hand still in my hair, and going home on the bus several people gave us "funny looks." Fortunately I was able to reach my stylist at home and he came right over with his tools and got poor Jerry loose. Jerry was very mad and said he's not going to date me again until I get some rollers that don't have this particular habit. I think he is being unfair, but he "means business." Can you help me?

FRANTIC
Buffalo

Dear Frantic Buffalo:

We're sorry to have to tell you that no rollers have yet been developed that do not occasionally catch the fingers of boys who tousle. The roller industry, however, is working very hard on the problem, as this complaint frequently comes up. Meanwhile why not ask Jerry to wear mittens? That way you'll be happy and he'll be safe.

There were many more, and perhaps the article even made a small contribution to Lady Bird's beautification program. But the point is this: once you've read that article you can never look at haircurlers again in quite the same way. You have been jolted by humor into looking with a fresh eye at something bizarre in our daily environment that was previously taken for granted. This is what the serious humorist is trying to do. The subject here isn't important—haircurlers certainly won't be the ruin of our society. But the method will work for subjects that *are* important, or for almost any subject, if you can find the right comic frame.

Over the last five years of the old *Life*, 1968–1972, I used humor to get at all kinds of subjects that might seem highly improbable. Quite a few columns were on the excesses of military power and procurement and on nuclear testing and radioactive leaks. One was on the petty squabbling over the shape of the table at the Vietnam peace conference in Paris. The situation had become so outrageous after nine weeks that it could only be approached through high ridicule, and I described various efforts to get peace at my own dinner table by changing its shape every night, or by lowering the chairs of different people to give them less "status," or by turning their chairs around so that the rest of us wouldn't have to "recognize" them. It was absurd, but hardly any more absurd than what was happening in Paris.

What made the pieces work as parody was that they stuck close to the form that they were parodying. Humor may seem to be an act of gross exaggeration. But the haircurler letters wouldn't succeed if we didn't recognize them as a specific journalistic form, both in their style and in their mentality.

Control is vital to humor. Don't use comical names like "Throckmorton." Don't repeat the same kind of joke two or three times—the reader will enjoy himself more if you only make it once. Trust the sophistication of readers who *do* know what you're doing, and don't worry about the rest.

The columns that I wrote for *Life* made people laugh. But they all had a serious purpose, which was to say: "Something grotesque is going on here—some erosion in the quality of life, or some threat to life itself, and yet everyone assumes that it's normal." Today in America the outlandish becomes routine overnight. The humorist is trying to say that it really is still outlandish.

I remember a cartoon by Bill Mauldin during the student turmoil of the late 1960s, when infantrymen and tanks were summoned to keep peace at a college in North Carolina and undergraduates at Berkeley were dispersed by a helicopter spraying them with Mace. The cartoon showed a mother pleading with her son's draft board: "He's an only child—please get him off the campus." It was Mauldin's way of pinning down this particular lunacy, and he was right on target. In fact, he was at the center of the bull's-eye, as Kent State and Jackson State subsequently proved.

Obviously the targets will change from week to week and from year to year. But there will never be a dearth of new lunacies—and dangers—for the humorist to detect and to fight. Lyndon Johnson in the years of his Vietnamization was brought down partly by Jules Feiffer and Art Buchwald. Joseph McCarthy and Spiro Agnew were brought down partly by Walt Kelly in the comic strip *Pogo*. H. L. Mencken brought down a whole galaxy of hypocrites in high places, and "Boss" Tweed was partly toppled by the cartoons of Thomas Nast.

Mort Sahl, a comic, was the only person who stayed awake during the Eisenhower years, when all of America was under sedation and didn't want to be roused. Many people regarded Sahl as a cynic, but he thought of himself as an idealist. "If I criticize somebody," he said, "it's because I have higher hopes for the world, something good to replace the bad. I'm not saying what the Beat Generation says: 'Go away because I'm not involved.' I'm here and I'm involved."

"I'm here and I'm involved"—make this your creed if you seriously want to write serious humor. The humorist operates on a deeper current than most people suspect. He must not only make a strong point; he must be willing to go against the grain, to state what the populace and the Presidents may not want to hear. Herblock and Art Buchwald perform an act of courage at least once a week. They say things which need to be said but which a regular columnist couldn't get away with. What saves them is that politicians are not known for humor and are therefore even more befuddled by it than the citizenry.

It is a lonely and perilous calling. No other kind of writer risks his neck so visibly on the high wire of public approval. It is the thinnest wire in all nonfiction, and the humorist knows that he will frequently fall off. Yet he is in dead earnest, this acrobat bobbing over our heads, trying to startle us with nonsense into seeing our lives with sense.

But of course humor has many uses besides the merely topical. They are not as urgent because they don't address problems of the day. But they are equally important because they help us to look at far older problems of the heart, the home, the job and all the other frustrations of just getting from morning to night.

In 1970 I interviewed the late Chic Young, creator of *Blondie,* when he had been writing and drawing that strip—daily and Sunday—for forty years, or 14,500 strips. It was the most popular of all comic strips, reaching 60 million readers in every corner of the world and in seventeen languages, and I asked him the secret of its durability.

"It's durable because it's simple," he said. "It's built on four things that everybody does: sleeping, eating, raising a family and making money." The comic twists on these four themes have been as various in the strip as they are in life. Dagwood's efforts to get money from his boss, Mr. Dithers, have their perpetual counterweight in Blondie's efforts to spend it. "I try to keep Dagwood in a world that people are used to," Young said. "He never does anything as special as playing golf, and the people who come to the door are just the people that an average family has to deal with."

I cite Young's four themes as a reminder that most humor, however freakish it may seem, is based on fundamental truths. Humor is not a separate organism that can survive on its own frail metabolism. It is a special angle of vision granted to certain writers who already write good English. They are not writing about life that is essentially ludicrous. They are writing about life that is essentially serious, but their vision focuses on the areas where serious hopes are mocked by some ironic turn of fate—"the strange incongruity," as Stephen Leacock put it, "between our aspiration and our achievement."

E. B. White also emphasizes that the humor writer is not some sort of maverick unrelated to the rest of the herd. "I don't like the word 'humorist,' never have," he says. "It seems to me misleading. Humor is a by-product that occurs in the serious work of some and not others. I was more influenced by Don Marquis than by Ernest Hemingway, by Perelman than by Dreiser."

Therefore I would suggest several principles for the writer of humor. Master the craft of writing good "straight" English; humorists from Mark Twain to Russell Baker are, first of all, superb writers. Don't search high and low for the outlandish and scorn what seems too ordinary; you will touch more chords by finding what is funny in what you know to be true. Finally, don't strain for laughs; humor is built on surprise, and you can surprise the reader only so often.

Unfortunately for the writer, humor is elusive and subjective. No two people think the same things are funny, and an article that one magazine will reject as a dud is often published by another that finds it hilarious. The reasons for rejection are also elusive. "It just doesn't work," editors say, and there's not much that they can add. Occasionally such a piece can be made to work—it has some flaw that can be repaired. Mortality, however, is high, and diagnosis generally futile. "Humor can be dissected, as a frog can," E. B. White once wrote, "but the thing dies in the process and the innards are discouraging to any but the pure scientific mind."

I'm no fancier of dead frogs, but I wanted to see if at least a few lessons could be learned by poking about in the innards, and I decided to teach a course at Yale in humor writing. I warned my students that I didn't think it had ever been tried, that quite possibly it couldn't be done, and that we might end up killing the thing we loved. Luckily, humor not only didn't die; it bloomed in the encircling desert of solemn term papers, and I subsequently taught the course again. Let me try briefly to reconstruct our journey.

"I hope to point out that American humor has an honorable literature," I wrote in a memo for prospective students, "and to consider the influence of certain pioneers on their successors. . . . Though the line between 'fiction' and 'nonfiction' is often fuzzy in humor, I see this as a nonfiction course—what you write will be based on external events. I am not interested in 'creative writing,' flights of pure imagination, and pointless whimsy."

I began by reading brief excerpts from early writers to show that a humorist can use a wide range of literary forms, or invent new ones. We started with George Ade's "Fables in Slang," the first of which appeared in 1897 in the *Chicago Record,* where Ade was a reporter. "He was just sitting unsuspectingly in front of a sheet of paper," Jean Shepherd writes in a fine introduction to his anthology, *The America of George Ade,* "when the innocent idea came to him to write something in fable form using the language and the clichés of the moment. In other words, slang. He said that to let people know that he knew better than to use slang in writing, he decided to capitalize all suspicious words and phrases. He was mortally afraid people would think he was illiterate."

He needn't have worried; by 1900 the Fables were so popular that he was earning $1,000 a week. Here, for instance, is "The Fable of the Subordinate Who Saw a Great Light":

Once there was an Employé who was getting the Nub End of the Deal. He kicked on the long Hours and the small Salary, and helped to organize a Clerks' Protective Association. He was for the Toiler as against the Main Squeeze.

To keep him simmered down, the Owners gave him an Interest. After that he began to perspire when he looked at the Pay-Roll, and it did seem to him that a lot of big, lazy Lummixes were standing around the shop doing the Soldier Act. He learned to snap his Fingers every time the Office Boy giggled. As for the faithful old Book-Keeper who wanted an increase to $9 and a week's Vacation in the Summer, the best he got was a little Talk about Contentment being a Jewel.

The saddest moment of the Day for him was when the whole Bunch knocked off at 6 o'clock in the Evening. It seemed a Shame to call 10 Hours a Full Day. As for the Saturday Half-Holiday Movement, that was little better than Highway Robbery. Those who formerly slaved alongside of him in the Galleys had to address him as Mister, and he had them numbered the same as Convicts.

One Day an Underling ventured to remind the Slave-Driver that once he had been the Friend of the Salaried Minion.

"Right you are," said the Boss. "But when I plugged for the lowly Wage-Earner I never had been in the Directors' Office to see the beautiful Tableau entitled 'Virtue copping out the Annual Dividend.' I don't know that I can make the situation clear to you, so I will merely remark that all those who get on our side of the Fence are enabled to catch a new Angle on this Salary Question."

Moral: *For Educational Purposes, every Employé should be taken into the Firm.*

The universal truth in that brief gem is still true eighty years later, as it is in almost all the Fables. "Ade was my first influence as a humorist," Perelman once said. "He had a social sense of history. His pictures of Hoosier life at the turn of the century are more documentary than any of those studies on how much people paid for their coal. His humor was rooted in a perception of people and places. He had a cutting edge and an acerbic wit that no earlier American humorist had."

Next I dipped into Ring Lardner, partly to demonstrate that dramatic dialogue, or the playlet, is another form that can serve the humorist. I'm a pushover for Lardner's nonsense plays, which he must have written just to amuse himself. But I suspect that he was also lampooning the holy conventions of playwriting, in which yards of italic type are used presumably to explain what's happening on stage. I share Lardner's obvious doubt that these stage directions are meant for anyone to read or to fathom.

My favorite Lardner play, *I Gaspiri (The Upholsterers)*, begins with the usual list of "Characters." I mean it is the usual list; they are not the usual characters:

Ian Obri, *a Blotter Salesman*
Johan Wasper, *his wife*
Greta, *their daughter*
Herbert Swope, *a nonentity*
Ffena, *their daughter, later their wife*
Egso, *a Pencil Guster*
Tono, *a Typical Wastebasket*

Act I consists of ten lines of dialogue, none of it involving these characters, and nine lines of irrelevant italic, concluding with: "The curtain is lowered for seven days to denote the lapse of a week." This leads into Act III, which, we are told, takes place on the Lincoln Highway with "two bearded glue lifters seated at one side of the road." This is followed by a long italic translator's note explaining the principal industry in Phlace, which is hoarding hay, whereupon the play concludes:

FIRST GLUE LIFTER: Well, my man, how goes it?
SECOND GLUE LIFTER: *(Sings "My Man," to show how it goes.)*

We savored this for the pleasure of nonsense as a humor form in itself, often masking some deeper annoyance on the part of the writer. Then I resurrected *Archy and Mehitabel,* by Don Marquis, to show that this influential humorist also used an unlikely medium—doggerel—for his message. Marquis, a columnist for the *New York Sun,* stumbled on a novel solution to the newspaperman's brutal problem of meeting a deadline and presenting his material in an orderly form, just as Ade stumbled on the fable. In 1916 he created the cockroach Archy, who banged out free verse on Marquis' typewriter at night, minus capital letters because he wasn't strong enough to press the shift key.

Archy's poems, describing his friendship with a cat named Mehitabel, are of a philosophical bent that one would not guess from their ragged appearance. No formal essay, for instance, could more thoroughly deflate all the aging actors who bemoan the current state of the theater than Marquis does in "The Old Trouper," a long poem in which Archy describes Mehitabel's meeting with an old theater cat named Tom:

> the stage is not what it
> used to be tom says
> he puts his front paw
> on his breast and says
> they don t have it any more
> they don t have it here
> the old troupers are gone
> there s nobody can troupe
> any more
> they haven t got it
> here . . .

Marquis uses humor to leaven his impatience with a type of bore that he knew well. It is of course a universal impatience, whatever the category of old-timer, just as it is a universal trait of old-timers to complain that their profession has gone to the dogs. Marquis achieves one of the classic functions of humor: to deflect anger into a channel where we can laugh at frailty instead of railing against it.

To illustrate parody I chose some passages from Thurber's nudge at Fowler's *Modern English Usage,* a book which, for all its eminence, can get (as Fowler would never allow me to say) mighty tiresome. Thurber has expressed with parody what I often have felt myself. Like Marquis, he has provided the humorist's gift of catharsis:

> The number of people who use "whom" and "who" wrongly is appalling. Take the common expression, "Whom are you, anyways?" That is of course, strictly speaking, correct—and yet how formal, how stilted! The usage to be preferred in ordinary speech and writing is "Who are you, anyways?" "Whom" should be used in the nominative case only when a note of dignity or austerity is desired. For example, if a writer is dealing with a meeting of, say, the British Cabinet, it would be better to have the Premier greet a new arrival, such as an under-secretary, with a "Whom are you, anyways?" rather than a "Who are you, anyways?"—always granted that the Premier is sincerely unaware of the man's identity. To address a person one knows by a "Whom are you?" is a mark either of incredible lapse of memory or inexcusable arrogance.

The next writers on my tour were Donald Ogden Stewart and Robert Benchley, two men who greatly broadened for their successors the possibilities of "free-association" humor, opening whole new territory. Typical of Stewart's reckless bravery—for the 1920s—is the opening of his book *The Crazy Fool:*

This is a story about a crazy fool named Charlie Hatch who inherited an insane asylum from his uncle. When he inherited the asylum, Charlie was 23 years old and in love, which made his total age 14 including depreciation and money for carfare and marbles.

Benchley was just as crazy a fool and perhaps even more daring, for he wrote in his own voice, adding a dimension of warmth and vulnerability that was not present in humorists like Ade and Marquis, who ducked into other forms such as fable and doggerel. Nobody has ever been better than Benchley at diving headlong into his subject:

> I have always tried to be as public-spirited as I could and yet save out a little time to myself for running and jumping. When the Fuel Administration wanted us all to save coal, I saved coal with a will; when it was Anti-Litter Week, I anti-littered; when the nation was supposed to be devoting itself to eating apples, I drank applejack until the cows came home—and very funny-looking cows they were, too.

> St. Francis of Assisi (unless I am getting him mixed up with St. Simeon Stylites, which might be very easy to do as both their names begin with "St.") was very fond of birds, and often had his picture taken with them sitting on his shoulders and pecking at his wrists. That was all right, if St. Francis liked it. We all have our likes and dislikes, and I have more of a feeling for dogs.

Perhaps they were all just paving the way for Perelman. In any case, Perelman gratefully acknowledged these debts. "You must learn by imitation," he said. "I could have been arrested for imitating Lardner in my pieces in *Judge* in the late 1920's— not the content, but the manner. These influences gradually fall away."

His own influence, however, has not been so easily shed. At his death in 1979 he had been writing steadily for more than half a century, putting the language through some of its most breathtaking loops, and in both America and England the woods are still full of writers and comics who were drawn into the gravitational pull of Perelman's style and never quite got back out. It doesn't take a detective to see his hand not only in such brilliant modern writers as Woody Allen and Marshall Brickman, but in the BBC's *Goon Show* and *Monty Python*, in the radio skits of Bob and Ray, and in the glancing wit of Groucho Marx—an influence more easily traceable because Perelman wrote several of the Marx Brothers' early movies.

What he created was an awareness that when the writer's mind works by free association it can ricochet from the normal to the absurd and, by the very unexpectedness of its angle, demolish whatever trite idea had been there before. To this element of perpetual surprise—after fifty years, Perelman's readers still never knew what was coming next—he grafted the dazzling wordplay that is his trademark, a vocabulary incredibly rich and recondite, and an erudition based on constant reading and travel. Still, even so rare a mixture would not have sustained him if he did not always have a target.

"All humor must be *about* something—it must touch concretely on life," he said, and though readers in their pure enjoyment of his style may lose sight of his deeper motive, some form of pomposity usually lies in ruins at the end of a Perelman piece, just as grand opera never quite recovered from the Marx Brothers, or banking from W. C. Fields. In the 1930s, Perelman recalled, "advertisers were giving themselves the most colossal airs, bombinating away about the creative importance of what they were doing," and many of his early satires and parodies lanced the fatuous ad campaigns of that era. But he was never at a loss for charlatans and knaves, especially in the worlds of Broadway and Hollywood, merchandising, health, medicine, food, fashion, publishing and travel. He had a sure instinct for pretension and cupidity.

I still remember my exhilaration on first encountering Perelman's *New Yorker* pieces. They contained sentences unlike any that I had ever seen before, or even imagined, and they absolutely fractured me:

The whistle shrilled and in a moment I was chugging out of Grand Central's dreaming spires. I had chugged only a few feet when I realized that I had left without the train, so I had to run back and wait for it to start. . . . With only two hours in Chicago I would be unable to see the city, and the thought drew me into a state of composure. I noted with pleasure that a fresh coat of grime had been given to the Dearborn Street station, though I was hardly vain enough to believe that it had anything to do with my visit.

From the ostermoor where I was stretched out lazily, I murmured an inviting "Come in!"
"Come in!" I murmured invitingly. He entered shaking himself vigorously. There had been a heavy fall of talcum several hours before and as far as the ground could see the eye was white.

Women loved this impetual Irish adventurer who would rather fight than eat and vice-versa. One night he was chafing at The Bit, a tavern in Portsmouth, when he overheard a chance remark from a brawny gunner's mate in his cups. . . . The following morning the "Maid of Hull," a frigate of the line mounting 36 guns, out of Bath and into bed in a twinkling, dropped downstream on the tide, bound for Bombay, object matrimony. On her as passenger went my great-grandfather. . . . Fifty-three days later, living almost entirely on cameo brooches and the ptarmigan which fell to the ptrigger of his pfowling piece, he at last sighted the towers of Ishpeming, the Holy City of the Surds and Cosines, fanatical Mohammedan warrior sects.

Obviously I could go on (and on), just as I could quote at length from all the writers I introduced to my class, ending with

Woody Allen, certainly the most cerebral humorist around today. Allen's magazine pieces, collected in *Getting Even* and *Without Feathers,* constitute a body of written humor unique for being both intellectual and hilarious, probing not only his well-known themes of death and anxiety, but such overbearing academic disciplines and literary forms as philosophy, psychology, drama, Irish poetry and the explication of texts ("Hassidic Tales"). Nor is he buried solely in an interior world of scholarship and neurosis. "A Look at Organized Crime," a parody of all the articles ever written explaining the Mafia, is one of the funniest pieces I know, and "The Schmeed Memoirs"—the recollections of Hitler's barber—is the ultimate jab at the "good German" who was just doing his job:

> I have been asked if I was aware of the moral implications of what I was doing. As I told the tribunal at Nuremberg, I did not know that Hitler was a Nazi. The truth was that for years I thought he worked for the phone company. When I finally did find out what a monster he was, it was too late to do anything, as I had made a down payment on some furniture. Once, toward the end of the war, I did contemplate loosening the Führer's neck-napkin and allowing some tiny hairs to get down his back, but at the last minute my nerve failed me.

None of the brief samplings in this chapter can convey more than a glimmer of the immense output and artistry of these writers. Nevertheless I wanted my students to know that they were operating within a long tradition of good writing and considerable nerve. I wanted them to try their wings and to fly high.

For the first weeks I told them to write in one of the existing humor forms—parody, lampoon, etc.—and not to use "I" or to write from personal experience. I assigned the same topic to the entire class, bringing in some current absurdity that I had noticed in the newspaper, in a magazine or in my mail. My best hopes were realized. What the students wrote was funny, inventive and often surrealistic. They jumped boldly into free association, nonsense and surprise. They learned that it was possible to throw off the chains of logic and to have fun making a serious point within a given humor form. They were heavily under the influence of Woody Allen's throwaway non sequiturs ("For this the Rabbi bashes his head in, which, according to the Torah, is one of the most subtle methods of showing concern").

After about four weeks, fatigue set in. The students had found that they were capable of writing humor. But they had also found how tiring it is to sustain a weekly act of comic invention, writing in other voices and formats. It was time to slow down their metabolism—to start them writing in their own voice and about their own experience. I declared a moratorium on reading Woody Allen and said I would tell them when they could read him again. That moment never came.

I adopted the Chic Young principle—stick to what you know —and began to read from writers who use humor as a vein that runs quietly through their work and leaves a cumulative pleasure. One piece was E. B. White's "The Eye of Edna," in which White recalls waiting on his Maine farm for the actual arrival of Hurricane Edna while listening for several days to inane radio reports of its progress. It's a perfect essay, full of wisdom and gentle wit.

Another writer whose work I excavated was Stephen Leacock, a Canadian. I remembered him from my boyhood as hilarious, but was afraid that, as often happens in looking up old friends, he would turn out to be "comical" but not funny. On the contrary, his pieces had survived the erosion of time, and one that I particularly remembered—"My Financial Career," in which he tries to open a bank account with $56—still seems the model piece of humor on how rattled we all become when dealing with banks, libraries and other institutions. Re-reading Leacock reminded me that still another function of the humorist is to represent himself as the victim or the dunce, helpless in most situations. This enables the reader to feel superior, or at least to identify with a fellow victim.

So that was the direction in which we now began to move, the students trying—often with difficulty—to find their "voice" and to write about their own lives. Many wrote about their families. We ran into problems, mainly of exaggeration, and gradually solved them, trying to achieve control—cutting the extra sentence, for instance, which explains a funny point that is already implicit.

A hard decision was to know how much exaggeration was allowable and how much was too much. One student wrote a funny piece about what a terrible cook his grandmother was. When I praised it he said that she was really a very good cook. I said I was sorry to hear it—somehow the piece now seemed less funny. He asked if this made a difference. I said it didn't make a difference in this piece, since I had enjoyed it without knowing it was untrue, but that I thought he would last longer as a humorist if he started from the truth rather than from invention. In Thurber's story "The Night the Bed Fell," we know that he has slightly enlarged the facts; but we also know that *something* happened to the bed that night in the attic.

In short, our class began by striving first for humor and hoping to wing a few truths along the way. We ended by striving for truth and hoping to add humor along the way. Ultimately we realized that the two are intertwined.

Near the end of the term, Perelman came and talked to the class, giving us more to ponder, needless to say, than I can summarize here. But I'll leave the last word to him.

"When you endeavor to be funny in every line," he said, "you place an intolerable burden not only on yourself but on the reader. You have to allow the reader to breathe. Whenever George S. Kaufman saw three straight funny lines in a play that he was directing, he cut the first two.

"The fact is that all of us have only one personality, and we wring it out like a dish towel. I don't think you can constantly create a new identity if you're a comic writer. You are who you are."

Sources

Most of the material by other writers that I have quoted in these pages was first written for a magazine or a newspaper and was subsequently reprinted in a book. In general the source cited below is for the original hardcover edition of the book. Many of these editions are now out of print but are available in public libraries. In many other cases the book has been reprinted in paperback and is relatively easy to obtain.

As for the body of this book, it was written to be what it is— an informal textbook for students and laymen—and is not a collection of articles that have previously appeared. Two exceptions are Chapter 7, which was adapted from my article "Is It an O.K. Word, Usewise?" which ran in *Life* on Aug. 24, 1969, and Chapter 15, which is partly based on my article, "Why Johnny's Teachers Can't Write," in the *New York Times Magazine*, Nov. 12, 1978.

P 28–29. Preface by E. B. White to *A Basic Chicken Guide* by Roy E. Jones. Copyright 1944 by Roy E. Jones. Reprinted by permission of William Morrow & Co. Also appears in *The Second Tree from the Corner*. Harper & Bros., 1954.

P 29–30. "The Hills of Zion," by H. L. Mencken, from *The Vintage Mencken*, gathered by Alistair Cooke. Vintage Books (paper), 1955.

P 31–32. *Fear and Loathing in Las Vegas,* by Hunter S. Thompson. Random House, 1972.

P 32–34. *How to Survive in Your Native Land,* by James Herndon. Simon & Schuster, 1971. Reprinted by permission of Simon & Schuster, a Division of Gulf & Western Corporation.

P 36. *The Lunacy Boom,* by William Zinsser. Harper & Row, 1970.

P 39. *Pop Goes America,* by William Zinsser, Harper & Row, 1966.

P 60–64. *The Lunacy Boom.*

P 66. *Slouching Towards Bethlehem,* by Joan Didion. Farrar, Straus & Giroux, 1968, Copyright © 1966 by Joan Didion. Reprinted by permission of the publisher.

P 67. *Nixon Agonistes,* by Garry Wills. Houghton Mifflin, 1970. Reprinted by permission of the publisher.

P 68–69. *The Pick by Pierre,* by Paul O'Neil, *Life,* Nov. 23, 1962. © 1962 by Time Inc. Reprinted with permission.

P 69. "The Last Time I Played Rugby," by Richard Burton. From *The Observer* (London), Oct. 4, 1970.

P 72. *Nixon Agonistes.*

P 73. "Coolidge," by H. L. Mencken, from *The Vintage Mencken.*

P 73–74. *Pop Goes America.*

P 85–87. *The Bottom of the Harbor,* by Joseph Mitchell. Little, Brown and Company, 1960. Reprinted by permission of Harold Ober Associates, Incorporated. © 1960 by Joseph Mitchell.

P 91–92. *Slouching Towards Bethlehem.*

P 92–93. *Coming into the Country,* by John McPhee. Farrar, Straus and Giroux, 1977.

P 94–95. *A Walker in the City,* by Alfred Kazin. Harcourt, Brace, 1951.

P 95–97. *No Room in the Ark,* by Alan Moorehead. Reprinted by permission of Harper & Row, Publishers, Inc.

P 97–98. *The Offensive Traveller,* by V. S. Pritchett. Alfred A. Knopf, 1964.

P 99–100. *Of a Fire on the Moon,* by Norman Mailer. Little, Brown and Company, 1971. © 1969, 1970 by Norman Mailer. By permission of the publisher.

P 116–118. "Brain Signals in Test Foretell Action," Feb. 13, 1971, by Harold M. Schmeck, Jr. © 1971 by the New York Times Company. Reprinted by permission.

P 119. "The Mystery of Memory," by Will Bradbury. *Life,* Nov. 12, 1971. © 1971, Time Inc. Reprinted with permission.

P 120. *Eleven Blue Men and Other Narratives of Medical Detection,* by Berton Roueché. Little, Brown and Company, 1954.

P 121–122. *Beyond Habitat,* by Moshe Safdie. The M.I.T. Press, 1970.

P 122–123. *The Immense Journey,* by Loren Eiseley. Random House, 1957.

P 123. *The Lives of a Cell: Notes of a Biology Watcher,* by Lewis Thomas. Viking Press, 1974.

P 139–140. "Hub Fans Bid Kid Adieu," by John Updike. From *Assorted Prose,* by John Updike. Alfred A. Knopf, 1965.

P 141. *Fields of Force: Fischer and Spassky at Reykjavik,* by George Steiner. Viking Press, 1974.

P 143. *Life on the Run,* by Bill Bradley. Quadrangle/The New York Times Book Co., 1976.

P 144. "In Indiana, The Roar of the Motor Is the Sweetest Sound," May 26, 1974, by Jean Shepherd. © 1974 by the New York Times Company. Reprinted by permission.

P 150–151. *Agee on Film,* by James Agee. McDowell Obolensky, 1958.

P 151–152. *Living-Room War,* by Michael J. Arlen. Viking Press, 1969.

P 153. *The Musical Scene,* by Virgil Thomson. Alfred A. Knopf, 1945.

P 154. *Ibid.*

P 155–156. "Virginia Woolf," Nov. 5, 1972, by Michael Rosenthal. © 1972 by the New York Times Company. Reprinted by permission.

P 160–161. *The Haircurl Papers,* by William Zinsser. Harper & Row, 1964.

P 167. *The America of George Ade,* edited, with an introduction by Jean Shepherd. G. P. Putnam's Sons, 1961.

P 168–169. *Shut Up, He Explained,* a Ring Lardner Selection. Charles Scribner's Sons, 1962.

P 169. *Archy and Mehitabel,* by Don Marquis. Doubleday & Co., 1927.

P 170. *The Owl in the Attic and Other Perplexities,* by James Thurber. Harper & Bros., 1931.

P 171. *The Crazy Fool,* by Donald Ogden Stewart. Albert & Charles Boni, 1925.

P 171. *Benchley—or Else!,* by Robert C. Benchley. Harper & Bros., 1947.

P 173. *Strictly from Hunger,* by S. J. Perelman. Random House, 1937. Also in *The Most of S. J. Perelman,* Simon & Schuster, 1958.

P 174. *Getting Even,* by Woody Allen. Random House, 1971.

Index